АЭРОФЛОТ

ИЛ-86

СССР-98459

СССР-42523

АЭРОФЛОТ

T0317843

BRUNO VANDERMUEREN

АЭРОФЛОТ

AEROFLOT
FLY SOVIET

FUEL

CONTENTS

AEROFLOT

ЛЕТАЙТЕ САМОЛЕТАМИ АЭРОФЛОТА, ЭТО ВЫГОДНО И УДОБНО

Fly Aeroflot Airplanes, it's economical and convenient. Aeroflot advertising slogan. Leaflet, 1960.

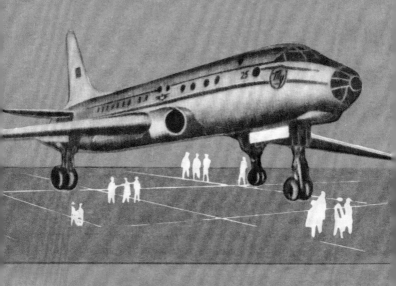

INTRODUCTION

In 1939, in a BBC radio broadcast, Winston Churchill described Soviet Russia as 'a riddle wrapped in a mystery inside an enigma'. The same could be said of Aeroflot, the Soviet Union's only airline, which to some degree served as a microcosm of the country itself. Following World War II, geopolitical tensions between the USSR and the US increased as the Cold War between the Eastern and Western blocs escalated. Secrecy and propaganda proliferated, with anything originating in the USSR, including its airline, regarded as deeply suspect by the West.

With an area of just over 8.5 million square miles, the USSR was by far the largest nation in the world (being more than twice the size of the US or Canada, at 3.8 million square miles each). Covering almost a sixth of the earth's land surface, it stretched more than 4,500 miles north to south and 6,200 miles east to west and encompassed eleven time zones. Given the inhospitable nature of much of that terrain, which included the unforgiving expanses of Siberia, it made no practical or economic sense to construct a comprehensive network of roads and railways across it. Consequently, the USSR was destined to embrace aviation.

Aeroflot (literally meaning Air Fleet) was officially defined in Article 10 of the USSR Air Code as 'a civil aviation organisation subordinate to the USSR Ministry of Civil Aviation'. But in practice Aeroflot was never a monolith. Under the unifying umbrella of the ministry, the airline's organisational structure expanded alongside its network, with a growing number of directorates usually tied to specific territories and each fulfilling its individual role within the overarching operation. By the time of Aeroflot's demise, with the fall of Communism in 1991, there were 33 directorates.

By the late 1930s, Aeroflot had the largest fleet of aircraft in the world, most of them small Polikarpov biplanes. Its growth was severely slowed by World War II, but increased rapidly from the mid-1950s. In 1958, the volume of passengers it carried surpassed that of American Airlines, then the world leader in passenger numbers.

While the total tally of Soviet air travellers was always second to that of all the American airlines combined, as the only airline in the USSR, Aeroflot held the distinction of being the world's biggest air carrier until the dissolution of the state in 1991. As an inseparable part of the Soviet political system, Aeroflot followed expansion targets set through government-ordained five-year plans rather than

ПАМЯТКА ПАССАЖИРА

previous page: **Passenger Notice**. Estonian SSR, 1976.

above: **Fly by 'Aeroflot' planes to the USSR!** Postcard, c.1960.

right: Ticket folder. A paper wallet used for tickets, passenger-information leaflets, postcards, stationery and luggage labels, c.1960.

being driven by a profit-based market economy.

A vital element in an extensive public-transport system, air travel in the USSR became popular in the late 1950s, with ticket prices dropping from the prohibitive rates of the early days to around the level of a train or bus fare. In the West airfares were mostly not reduced until much later, following the introduction of economy-class cabins and low-cost carriers (although Pacific Southwest Airlines operated a low-cost service within California from 1949).

Soviet civil aviation of the 1920s mainly relied on German Junkers aircraft but the 1930s saw the rise of Soviet domestic production, with aircraft such as the K-4 and K-5, the ANT-9 and the Stal-2 and Stal-3 (designed by Kalinin, Tupolev and Putilov, respectively). The Lisunov Li-2, a Soviet version of the Douglas DC-3 Dakota, dominated the sky in the 1940s. From the early 1950s, Aeroflot operated only aircraft and helicopters built in the Soviet Union and Eastern European Communist states. In 1952, the British de Havilland Comet, the first commercial jet airliner, revolutionised air travel. But after a number of catastrophic accidents, the USSR seized the lead in fast passenger jet transport with the introduction of the Tupolev Tu-104

in 1956. Within five years, the Soviet aviation industry would produce a whole range of new airliners and helicopters named after their famous designers: Tupolev, Ilyushin, Antonov, Yakovlev, Mil and Kamov.

Passenger numbers continued to soar, and by the mid-1960s almost one in five air travellers was on an Aeroflot flight. By then, the fleet had already expanded to over 7,000 aircraft and helicopters. By the early 1970s, the Soviet airline was also transporting about a sixth of the world's air cargo. In 1976, it became the first airline to carry more than a hundred million passengers a year, serving some 3,600 destinations.

The scale of operations and the diversity of its activities set Aeroflot apart from other airlines. By the time of its fiftieth anniversary in 1973, on a typical summer's day, 'Aerograd' or 'the Soviet city in the sky', as the span of Aeroflot operations was often referred to, might be populated by some 400,000 passengers and carry more than 6,000 tons of machinery and other cargo. In addition, there were flying farmers spraying crops, flying fishermen scouting for schools of fish and flying doctors bringing emergency medical aid. There were flights for geological prospecting, forest patrols and pipeline

Летайте в СССР самолетами Аэрофлота

inspections. Yet other planes were guiding ships through the Great Northern Sea Route or providing supplies to Pole Stations. These were just some of the daily tasks undertaken by Aeroflot to aid the development of the national economy.

The airline's ever-growing workforce (by 1970 there were some 400,000 employees, of whom 25,000 were pilots) was responsible for all aspects of operations: air-traffic control, aircraft maintenance, fuelling, airports and ground handling, ticketing, staff training and certification, medical services and staff housing. Aeroflot was also of political importance, with its flights forming a crucial link with and between the Soviet satellite states. In addition, it had a role within the military as a transport reserve for the Soviet Air Force.

Until the mid-1970s, each type of aircraft in the fleet had its own livery, but in 1973, to increase recognition of Aeroflot's corporate identity worldwide, the Ministry of Civil Aviation introduced a standard livery for all planes. In the new design, a white fuselage was bisected by a bold blue horizontal cheatline running the length of the windows, with light grey underneath, a large Soviet flag on the tail and prominent 'Aeroflot' lettering and logo. A variation with bright red replacing blue was used in the polar regions for better visibility against the snowy landscape.

left: **Fly to the USSR by Aeroflot**. Promotional booklet presenting Aeroflot's main routes, c.1960.

above: Flight attendant Tatyana Zinchenko on the cover of Aeroflot's inflight magazine *Soviet Airlines*, No.3, 1977. In the background, an Ilyushin Il-62M in the standard livery introduced after 1973.

above: Aeroflot ticket office, 33 Avenue des Champs-Elysées, Paris, 1970s.

right: **Aeroflot, Fly – Fast, Profitable, Convenient. Inquiries and ticket sales at all airports and Aeroflot agencies in the USSR and abroad**. Pocket calendar depicting an Il-18, 1961.

Outside the USSR, Soviet airliners were often regarded as unsafe and uneconomical – as inferior imitations of their Western counterparts. In fact, however, the Soviets successfully developed many airliners and helicopters in accordance with stringent regulations to meet the specific requirements of Aeroflot operations. These aircraft proved to be reliable machines, in many ways comparable with their counterparts in the West, if fundamentally different in design approach. From the mid-1950s on, the safety record of Soviet airliners gradually improved and became akin to that of the West, contradicting a persistent reputation for poor safety.

In broad terms, Soviet aircraft were adapted to suit airport conditions, while in the West airports were adapted to accommodate aircraft. Soviet terrain, which included often unpaved runways, along with a lack of specialised ground-handling equipment, created the need for heavier, more robust and self-reliant airliners. However, this entailed the sacrifice of some degree of payload or range.

The All-Union Department for Aviation Equipment Exports and Imports (known as AVIAEXPORT) was established in 1961. This body was responsible for the export of planes and helicopters, their maintenance equipment and after-sales service. Rapid growth saw AVIAEXPORT become an All-Union Foreign Trade Organisation in 1964. By 1980, more than 4,000 civil planes and helicopters had been exported to 55 countries, mainly in Eastern Europe but including Cuba and a number of African and Asian nations.

АЭРОФЛОТ

ЛЕТАТЬ –
БЫСТРО,
ВЫГОДНО,
УДОБНО

Справки и продажа билетов
во всех аэропортах и агентствах
Аэрофлота в СССР и за границей

Aeroflot. Postcard depicting the Antonov An-10, c.1960.

In order to sell aircraft to 'Western' countries, Soviet manufacturers were required to comply with Western aviation regulations, an expensive and time-consuming process, requiring the construction of specially adapted export models. Furthermore, the political climate of the Cold War, in combination with operational and economic challenges, made Western airlines reluctant to purchase Soviet planes (apart from a few short-lived exceptions). As a result, Aeroflot was not only the first customer of every new Soviet airliner, but also the sole operator of some types, a fact that greatly contributed to its unique character.

Despite the Soviet economic stagnation of the 1980s, Aeroflot traffic continued to increase. In 1990, the last complete year before the dissolution of the USSR, Aeroflot transported some 3 million tons of freight, 97.6 per cent of it within the USSR. In addition, it carried 137,198,200 passengers, about an eighth of the world's total, though because of restrictions on freedom of movement 96.77 per cent of these flew on domestic flights. In previous decades the proportion of passengers on international flights had been even lower, at 2.5 per cent in 1980 and only 0.6 per cent in 1960. Outside the Soviet Union, what the world had seen of Aeroflot was just the tip of the iceberg.

above: **Born in October, Created by the October Revolution**. Promotional poster, c.1977, celebrating the 60th anniversary of the October Revolution. The top section of the poster shows the civil aviation flag, on top of which are the emblems of the Order of Lenin and the October Revolution. Underneath, an Aeroflot Ilyushin Il-62M flies over the cruiser Aurora, the Peter and Paul Fortress and the Kremlin, symbols of the 1917 Great October Revolution.

overleaf: **Map, flight routes of Aeroflot**. Early post-war routemap, c.1947. (Note the double notation 'Königsberg – Kaliningrad' after the city had become part of the Soviet Union and was renamed in 1946.)

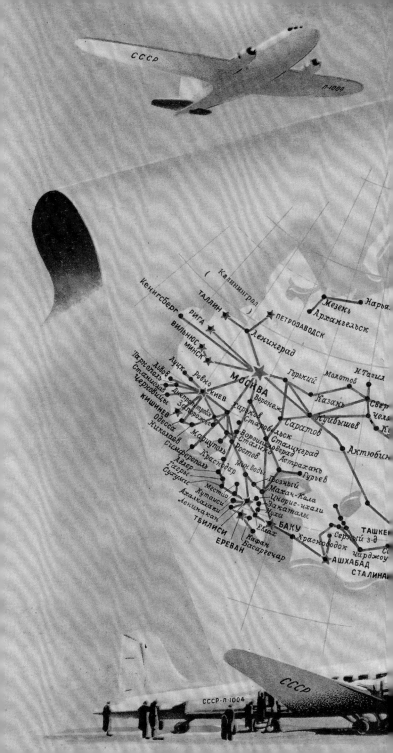

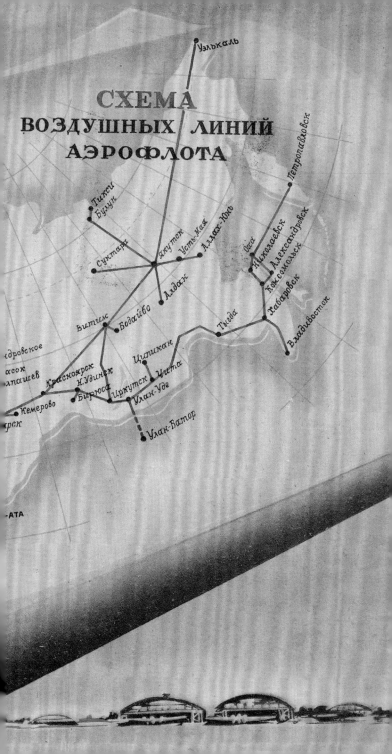

СХЕМА ВОЗДУШНЫХ ЛИНИЙ АЭРОФЛОТА

1. BEGINNINGS

Aviation at the end of the Russian empire

Of all the twentieth century's remarkable inventions, none has exerted such a powerful and lasting influence on the human imagination as the aeroplane.

On the morning of Sunday 25 July 1909, French aviator Louis Blériot, in his Blériot XI, became the first to fly across the English Channel. The excitement at his achievement spread quickly across Europe and the rest of the world, including to Russia, where the press were no less lyrical in their praise than the French or British. In the following months, French aviators gave public demonstrations of their 'heavier than air' flying machines across the European continent.

On 15 September that same year, thousands of curious Muscovites flocked to Khodynka field, just outside the city, to witness the first flight of an aeroplane in Russia, as French aviator Georges Legagneux gave a successful demonstration of his Voisin biplane. Four days later he repeated the feat, and subsequent performances in St Petersburg and Odessa attracted even larger numbers of enthusiastic spectators.

Imperial Russia was the least industrialised and most widely illiterate of the major European powers, making it an unlikely place for a technological revolution. Despite this, aviation soon occupied a prominent position in the cultural landscape. By the end of 1909, several major cities, including St Petersburg, Moscow, Odessa and Kiev, had their own private aeronautical organisations. The passion for flight intensified when on 8 March 1910 Russian aviator Mikhail Efimov gave a display in a French Farman IV biplane in the Black Sea port of Odessa.

The underdeveloped state of the Russian industry, combined with a lack of private investment (a vital factor in the rapid growth of the American and European aviation industries), meant Russia was dependent on European manufacturers for aircraft parts. Nevertheless, a number of Russians began to build their own aeroplanes, most notably Yakov Gakkel and Igor Ivanovich Sikorsky, who was to become Imperial Russia's greatest aircraft designer.

By spring 1913, Sikorsky had constructed the world's first (and largest) multi-engine aircraft, named the Russian Knight. A major accomplishment for Russia's nascent aviation industry, it was capable of transporting twelve people, including a two-man crew, and could

The giant Russian Knight, 1913. On the right of its remarkable viewing platform stands its designer, Igor Sikorsky. In the centre is Baron Alexander Vasilyevich Kaulbars, Russian General of the Imperial Army, famous explorer of Central Asia and one of the first organisers of the Russian Imperial Air Force.

stay in the air for several hours at speeds of around 50 mph. In early 1914, Sikorsky presented his latest, even larger creation, the Ilya Muromets. Named after Russia's beloved folk hero, it had a cabin with electric lighting and heating as well as chairs, tables and a sleeping compartment for passenger comfort. An observation platform was situated on top of the fuselage behind the wing and alongside that – another first – was a toilet.

Having set several world records for payload and flight duration, on 30 June the aircraft took off on a round trip between St Petersburg and Kiev. Political tensions had been escalating throughout Europe, and two days before the flight, Archduke Franz Ferdinand of Austria was assassinated in Sarajevo, an event that became a catalyst for World War I. The Ilya Muromets was due to begin passenger flights that same year, but instead was adapted for military use. Although the aircraft were successfully employed as the world's first heavy bombers, they were unable to turn the tide of the conflict. In February 1917, long-standing discontent with the monarchy together with hardships suffered during the war led to the first Russian revolution. The empire collapsed and in the Great October Revolution later that year the Bolsheviks seized power. By the time World War I officially ended on 11 November 1918, Russia had descended into civil war.

By 1920, the Bolshevik Red Army had defeated the majority of the White forces and other rivals (including the former Allied forces of World War I, who were supporting the Whites). The Bolshevik Communist Party swiftly reorganised into the world's first socialist republic.

Years of war, both international and civil, had almost completely destroyed Russian industry, including aircraft production. Factory workers fled to the countryside as the cities threatened to disintegrate under the pressures of famine and violent unrest. Simultaneously, punitive measures were deployed by the new elite against anyone designated a counter-revolutionary element, including scientists, designers and engineers. Some were arrested or killed, while others escaped abroad – among them Igor Sikorsky, who was to become America's most famous helicopter designer.

On 17 January 1921, the Council of the People's Commissariat, headed by Vladimir Lenin, passed a resolution 'On air traffic over the territory of the RSFSR [USSR] and its territorial waters'. Thus for the first time the Russian state declared sovereignty over its airspace. This important landmark provided a legal basis for the development of civil aviation and regular air connections with other countries.

On 1 May 1921, following the establishment of the Chief Administration of the Civil Air Fleet, an inaugural 500-mile air route was opened from Kharkov (now Kharkiv in Ukraine) to Moscow, via Kursk, Orel and Tula. Flights took place twice a week using six of Sikorsky's Ilya Muromets aeroplanes – all that remained of a fleet of more than 80 built during the war. Flights departing simultaneously from Kharkov and Moscow met half way in Orel, where cargo and passengers were exchanged. After refuelling, each returned to its respective base. At last, the Ilya Muromets was being used as originally intended – as a passenger plane.

These aeroplanes had been punishingly tested during their wartime service and alarming incidents became commonplace. On one occasion, the far-right engine caught fire and the mechanic crawled along the wing to extinguish the flames using his leather jacket – after which, running on its three remaining engines, the plane successfully completed its flight. Between 1 May and 10 October, 43 flights were undertaken, transporting a total of 60 passengers and more than 2 tons of cargo.

Postcard (in Russian and French), with a photograph of the Ilya Muromets, c.1925. The Dobrolet logo, designed by Alexander Rodchenko, appears on the bottom right corner and on the reverse side.

2. THE GERMAN CONNECTION

Deruluft and Junkers Luftverkehr Russland

Having been isolated by the other European powers and the US following World War I, Germany and Russia, once enemies, sought to strengthen their political and economic ties. By 1920, with the civil war drawing to a close, Soviet officials had begun to negotiate with Germany over the establishment of air routes, recognising that a fast and regular connection between their respective capitals would be in both their interests. The long train journey between Moscow and Berlin, typically taking 110 hours (almost five days), discouraged the efficient practice of both diplomacy and trade. In addition, the route passed through Poland – still an enemy of both countries – where strict border controls hampered the transport of freight as well as confidential diplomatic mail.

Deruluft (1922–37)
The solution to the problem came in the form of an airline founded jointly by Germany and Russia on 11 November 1921 and known as Deruluft (DEutsche-RUssische LUFTverkehrsgesellschaft).

The Soviet government bought ten Fokker F3 aircraft from Holland, which were registered RR1 to RR10 (RR standing for Russian Republic). These were single-engine planes with a cruising speed of 85 mph, an open cockpit and room for five passengers. Night flying was still technologically impossible and the distance of nearly 1,120 miles between Berlin and Moscow was too great for the Fokkers to cover in daylight hours. So Devau airport near Königsberg – Germany's easternmost city until it was subsumed into the Soviet Union in 1945 and renamed Kaliningrad – was chosen as the departure point. Night trains covered the journey between Berlin and Königsberg, with Deruluft cars and buses ferrying passengers between Königsberg railway station and the airfield. From here, the 750-mile flight, stopping at Kowno (now Kaunas) and Smolensk, reached Moscow in around nine hours, reducing the journey between the capitals to less than 24 hours.

The service was officially opened on 1 May 1922, with flights departing simultaneously from Moscow and Königsberg twice a week. It was the longest and most arduous air route in Europe. Equipped with only a compass, a tachometer (the plane had no speed gauge) and a route map, pilots flew at low altitude, using rivers, roads and railways to navigate. The two Fokkers, moving in opposite directions,

Fokker F3 RR-10 (top) and RR-3 (bottom). Both these planes flew in Deruluft service from 1922 until October 1928 when they were transferred to the Red Air Force flight school.

would pass each other near Vitebsk, where passengers and crew were often able to exchange a wave. The service carried diplomatic couriers as well as regular passengers, freight and mail.

Restricted by weather conditions and daylight hours, flights operated only between 1 May and 31 October, a six-month period named the 'summer season', a term still used across the industry today. Even so, the airfields at Smolensk and Kaunas often turned to mud in bad weather, with conditions at Kaunas frequently so treacherous that damage to landing gear was a regular occurrence. It therefore became policy to fill the fuel tanks to maximum capacity and reduce the payload by around 220 lbs so the planes could fly non-stop. This made the journey between Smolensk and Königsberg, at 510 miles, the longest flight leg in the world.

In total, Deruluft made around a hundred scheduled flights in 1922, carrying 338 passengers, 2,308 lbs of mail and 38,690 lbs (over 17 tons) of freight and luggage. The number of flights continued to increase each year, so that on 7 August 1925 the airline was able to celebrate 1 million kilometres of flight.

On 1 May 1926, German airline Lufthansa opened one of the first night-time air routes in the world, linking Berlin and Königsberg and thus further shortening the journey time between Berlin and Moscow. Guiding searchlights were installed on the ground every 15 to 18 miles, with auxiliary red spotlights at 3- to 5-mile intervals. Over time, however, the alliance between the two countries became less stable and the Soviets began to suspect German pilots of being involved in espionage and smuggling. This led the Soviet authorities to ban Deruluft's Russian pilots from flying between Königsberg and Berlin, while flights by German pilots were always observed as they crossed Soviet territory. There was an assigned checkpoint that had to be flown over at the border and the entire route was monitored to ensure there were no deviations. In-flight photography was forbidden and German pilots were kept under surveillance during their stay in Moscow.

Two years later, on 7 June 1928, Deruluft opened a second route between Leningrad (St Petersburg) and Riga (Latvian SSR) via Reval (now Tallinn, Estonia). In 1933, the year the Nazis seized power in Germany, the airline began operating winter flights between Moscow and Berlin and the section between Moscow and Velikiye Luki (280 miles westbound) was equipped for night flights. The route from Leningrad was extended in 1935 so it too reached as far as Königsberg. By this time, Deruluft ran thirteen aircraft, nine of them German (three Junkers F 13s, two Rohrbach Rolands and four Ju-52/3ms) and four of them Soviet-built ANT-9s. In 1936, the airline's last full year of operation, it carried 13,689 passengers, 495 tons of freight

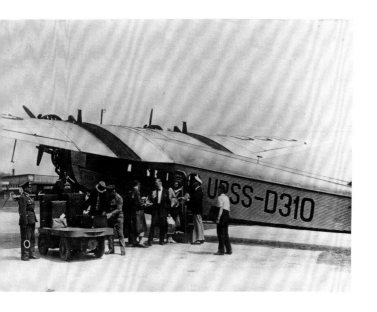

Passengers boarding the flight from Berlin to Moscow. This Tupolev ANT-9 URSS-D310 was named after the Soviet city of Orel and served with Deruluft from 1933 until it was transferred to Aeroflot in July 1936.

and luggage and 100 tons of mail. But worsening political relations between Nazi Germany and the USSR led the Soviets to terminate the contract and dissolve the airline, with all flights ceasing on 31 March 1937.

Junkers Luftverkehr Russland (1922–25)

A second airline, the German Junkers Luftverkehr, had signed a contract on 6 February 1922 – not long after the foundation of Deruluft – to operate flights in Russia under the name Junkers Luftverkehr Russland. In November, the company agreed to open a Junkers aircraft- and engine-production facility in the Moscow suburb of Fili. With Russia's aircraft industry in ruins after the civil war and Germany's production heavily restricted by the Treaty of Versailles, it seemed an excellent opportunity for both nations – but the co-operation proved short-lived.

Three all-metal four-seater Junkers 13s were rented from Junkers Luftverkehr Russland to fly from Moscow to Nizhny Novgorod during the annual summer trade fair, operating under the name Aviakultura.

A Suggestion for this Summer

An Air Excursion to **MOSCOW**

Travel brochure promoting the use of Deruluft air transport to Moscow and Leningrad, c.1935-36.
Interior text reads: **The Triumph of Speed! Just think, starting on your return trip from Moscow at 8 in the morning, arriving the very same day at 8.20 in the evening in Paris – this is indeed a sensation, a thrilling experience worthy of a Jules Verne. Berlin – Danzig – Königsberg – Kaunas – Moscow, 1,682 km or 10 hours. Single fare 160 Reichsmark or $64. Berlin – Riga – Tallinn – Leningrad, 1,679 km or 9 ½ hours. Single fare 140 Reichsmark or $56.**

The 260-mile route, piloted exclusively by German crews, was opened on 1 August 1922. By the end of September, after both the fair and flights had come to an end, a total of 57 flights had transported 209 passengers and 5,805 lbs of cargo, mainly consisting of newspapers.

A year later, on 1 June 1923, Junkers Luftverkehr established the then longest air route in the USSR: between Moscow and Baku (in Azerbaijan SSR) via Kharkov, Rostov, Novorossiysk, Batumi and Tiflis. This was part of an even grander plan for a transcontinental airline connecting Sweden and Persia. Flying largely over open water, the service was initially irregular and risky; when the route was changed, flights to Baku continued until 1 October. However, as it proved impossible to recover costs, all regular flights for the following year were cancelled and only a chartered service remained. Contractual disputes led to the early demise of the Junkers production plant at Fili and by May 1925 the airline had ceased operations.

top: Luggage label, early 1930s, depicting a Dornier Merkur aircraft flying both of the main Deruluft routes.

bottom: **Deruluft / Berlin / Moscow / Leningrad / Deruluft**. Luggage label bearing the company logo, early 1930s.

Junkers Caramel. Sweet wrapper depicting a Junkers airplane, late 1920s.

Aviator. Sweet wrapper by the Krasny Oktyabr (Red October) confectionery factory, Moscow, late 1920s.

3. AEROFLOT'S FORGOTTEN ANCESTORS

Dobrolet, Ukrvozdukhput and Zakavia

The foundations for the first entirely Soviet airline were laid on 9 February 1923 with the establishment of a permanent Civil Aviation Council, subordinate to the Chief Administration of the Workers' and Peasants' Red Air Fleet (called Glavvozdukhflot, essentially the Air Force). This date is celebrated as the birthday of Soviet civil aviation and, by extension, of Aeroflot.

Dobrolet (1923–30)

The nascent Soviet Republic required large financial resources to create an airline, as well as to establish an aircraft-production industry. To stimulate the economy, head of government Vladimir Lenin had introduced the New Economic Policy (NEP), drawing on private investment to enable a limited form of capitalism. On 17 March 1923, in accordance with this policy, an airline was launched: the Voluntary Air Fleet Society or Dobrolet. With the state retaining a controlling stake, the financial risks of the enterprise were underwritten by the government, and in return the airline was subject to the rule of the Civil Aviation Council. A commercial air fleet was also seen as a useful reserve for the Red Air Fleet in the event of war.

An agreement was signed with Germany for the purchase of fourteen Junkers F 13s, along with spare parts. Dobrolet was helped by the recently founded Society of Friends of the Air Fleet (Obshchestvo Druzey Vozdushnogo Flota) to raise funds for the aircraft, airfield construction and the establishment of air routes. The Society organised pleasure and propaganda flights over the central airfield in Moscow, generating publicity for the acquisition of shares. In preparation for the launch of future routes, planes flew to several Soviet cities where rallies were co-ordinated to show support for the formation of a powerful Soviet air fleet. Inhabitants of surrounding villages were gathered at each airfield, sometimes a day in advance, and there was genuine interest in catching a glimpse of the aircraft.

Aeronautical themes were introduced into the creative arts – from textiles, ceramics and architecture to film, theatre and painting – and prominent contemporary artists were commissioned to work on large-scale advertising campaigns. This propaganda was so successful that just three months after its creation, the Society had almost 200,000 members, and within a year almost a million.

Dobrolet's identity and advertising were developed by leading

top: **Dobrolet passenger flights in Central Asia. Buy Dobrolet shares. Central-Asian Directorate Dobrolet, Tashkent**. Poster, 1923, artist B. Lavrenov.

bottom: Group photograph with a Dobrolet Junkers F 13, c.1930.

Constructivist artist Alexander Rodchenko, who was appointed as the main designer for the airline's posters, working with his friend, the poet Vladimir Mayakovsky. On 3 July 1923, Mayakovsky made his first flight on board a Deruluft Fokker F3, alongside his lover Lilya and her husband, writer and critic Osip Brik (who accepted his wife's infidelities). Following this experience, he wrote the poem Moscow-Königsberg: '... Five climbed in / The earth fell away / Paths scattered ...' Basing his design on a sketch by pioneering abstract artist Kazimir Malevich, Rodchenko also created several Dobrolet logos that were used across newspapers and journals and on stationery, lapel pins and membership badges.

At the beginning of the 20th century, Russia remained largely illiterate, which meant the Communist Party had to rely on strong visual imagery to communicate its ideological messages. Posters advertising subscriptions for Dobrolet's shares were aggressive in style, with slogans that played to a sense of guilt and duty rather than to aspirations or desires. By linking a citizen's sense of personal responsibility and community to efforts to support Dobrolet and the Red Air Fleet, the posters invoked the underlying purpose of fulfilling the Communist Party's plan to reshape Soviet society. Largely thanks to this advertising campaign, the share capital of Dobrolet increased from 2 million to 5 million rubles over the course of 1923.

As with the flights of Aviakultura in 1922, Dobrolet's first route was from Moscow (Khodynka airport) to the trade fair in Nizhny Novgorod. From 1 August 1923, the 260-mile route, with its intermediate stop at Ivanovo-Voznesensk, operated three times a week. Dobrolet hired German crews from the Junkers company while more Russian pilots were trained. Despite a high ticket price of 70 rubles, flights sold out in advance. By 22 September, when the trade fair ended and the service closed, 94 flights had transported 229 passengers and almost 2 tons of mail and other cargo.

Flying at an altitude of 800 feet without radio or telegraph communication, pilots navigated via landmarks, rivers and railways and so needed a thorough knowledge of the route, its airfields and its landing sites. In the event of a technical problem, they were instructed to land close to the railway line so stranded passengers could be picked up by train.

In its first year, Dobrolet extended its operations to the five Soviet Central Asian republics of Kazakhstan, Uzbekistan, Turkmenistan, Kyrgystan and Tajikistan, whose borders were still in dispute. In November 1923, Dobrolet sent three Junkers aircraft by rail from Moscow to Tashkent in the Uzbek SSR: two months later, following an uprising in Khorezm, the planes were commissioned by the Red Air Force and their passenger seats replaced with bomb racks and

top: Dobrolet logos designed by Alexander Rodchenko, 1923. *LEF* magazine, No.2 (April-May), 1923.

bottom: **Today I will add 1 ruble to Dobrolet, Prombank** (Industrial Bank), **Gosbank** (State Bank) **and become a shareholder of Dobrolet.** 1920s.
left: Poster, right: Back cover of *Wings of Yakutia*, published by Dobrolet, 1925 .

above: **Airplane**. Sweet wrapper, Promkonditer factory, Arkhangelsk.

right: **Dobrolet**. Sweet wrapper, late 1920s.

machine guns. From its inception, therefore, Soviet civil aviation was inextricably linked with the military.

May 1924 saw the inauguration of the Central Asian passenger route. Starting from Tashkent, planes flew via Aulie Ata (now Taraz) and Pishpek (also formerly Frunze, now Bishkek), finally landing in Alma-Ata in the Kazakh SSR seven hours later – a great improvement on the gruelling eight-day horse ride. Other routes opened up in the same year, including one to Dushanbe in the Tajik SSR and an 285-mile route from Kagan to Khorezm in the Uzbek SSR, stopping at Chardzhou and Dargan Ata. This vanguard of Soviet progress meant citizens of Dushanbe saw their first aeroplane two years before the first car arrived in the region.

In those early years, routes were regularly changed or closed because of lack of passengers or problems caused by rebel groups, with each aircraft being equipped with two rifles and several hand grenades in case of an emergency landing in hostile territory. The terrain was a further challenge: pilots flew over mountainous areas and across stretches of desert with temperatures ranging from 50°C in summer to as low as minus 30°C in winter.

Dobrolet could not compete on price with train tickets so it made no sense to run the same routes as the railways. But Soviet Central

Asia had few roads and rail travel was in its infancy, with many lines still under construction. Camel caravans crossing the desert or horseback treks along mountain trails took at least ten days to cover the same distance as a Dobrolet plane could fly in just a few hours. In addition, the caravan routes were vulnerable to attacks from Basmachi rebels, including some who crossed the Afghan border into Tajik territory. There was therefore a greater demand for air transport in Central Asia than in any other part of the USSR.

On 1 June 1924, the flying season started with the re-opening of the Moscow to Nizhny Novgorod route. By the end of the month, this had been extended east as far as Kazan in Tartarstan, making a total distance of 509 miles. The Junkers were now joined by a single AK-1 aeroplane with capacity for two passengers. Designed by V. L. Aleksandrov and V. V. Kalinin, this was the first Soviet-built passenger plane used by Dobrolet. Although reliable, it was made almost entirely of wood and was slower than the more advanced four-seater Junkers.

Aerial photography flights were organised for map-making and new equipment was developed for agricultural dusting and spraying. In 1925, three aircraft equipped to spray agricultural pesticides received from the Air Force were sent to North Caucasia to battle locusts and mosquitoes. It was clear from the start that the Soviet authorities envisaged that its air fleet would fulfil many different roles.

By 28 March 1926, Dobrolet had flown a landmark 1 million kilometres and by 1927 it had surpassed Deruluft in traffic volume and route length. In 1929, the national prefix for aircraft registration was changed from RR (Russian Republic) to CCCP (Union of Soviet Socialist Republics), though all aircraft intended for flights outside the Soviet Union carried either the French prefix URSS (Union des Républiques Socialistes Soviétiques) or less frequently the English USSR (Union of Soviet Socialist Republics). Most such flights were to continental Europe, where French was the first language and France was the most advanced nation in the realm of aviation.

In May 1929, a 2,920-mile airmail service between Moscow and Irkutsk was established. Following the line of the Trans-Siberian railway, it was the first route in the USSR with sections equipped for night flights. This allowed an overall journey time of only 36 hours compared with six days by train.

The early aviators were adventurers who were hailed as genuine heroes. From the moment of take-off, they were cut off from the world, without radio communication or navigational instruments. In low cloud and rain they had no option but to fly close to the ground. Cabins were unpressurised, which meant that on flights over the high Pamir mountain ranges, such as the one from Gharm to Khorog in the Tajik SSR, everyone on board had to have special clothing and breathing equipment. Even today, this flight is recognised as one of the most difficult and dangerous in the world.

By 1929, the Soviet Civil Air Fleet had expanded to about 70 aircraft. The majority were still German Junkers and Dorniers, along with Dutch Fokkers. But there were also sixteen Kalinin K-4s, the first Soviet civil aircraft to go into production. A multi-purpose aircraft used for passenger transport, aerial photography and as an air ambulance, 39 K-4s were built in total.

Within weeks of Dobrolet's formation in March 1923, two other airlines had been founded in the USSR: Ukrvozdukhput, based in Kharkov, Ukraine, and Zakavia, based in Transcaucasia.

Zakavia (1923–25) and Ukrvozdukhput (1923–30)

The name Zakavia, derived from Zakavkazie (Russian for Transcaucasia), stands for Transcaucasian Air Transport Society. The airline consisted of two Junkers F 13s based in Tiflis (now Tbilisi, Georgia) and one in Baku (in Azerbaijan). On 8 January 1924, a weekly service was set up between these two cities. However, bad weather and lack of passengers resulted in repeated flight cancellations and by April the route was discontinued.

On 7 August, the airline launched sightseeing flights, including

To all ... To all ... To all ... One is not a citizen of the USSR, who is not a shareholder of Dobrolet. One gold ruble will make anyone a shareholder of Dobrolet. Poster by Alexander Rodchenko, 1923.

a short 37-mile route between Tiflis and the resort of Manglisi. These proved popular among tourists visiting the various sanatoria in the region.

The following year, however, a fire broke out on a flight from Tiflis to Sukhumi (in Abkhazia), probably originating in the passenger cabin. The plane went down, exploding on impact and killing all five people on board. As a result, the airline was disbanded and its facilities merged into Ukrvozdukhput.

Ukrvozdukhput (meaning Ukrainian Airline Company) was founded on 26 March 1923, with six all-metal four-seater Dornier Komet II aircraft delivered from Germany. The shipment was late, which meant flights were postponed until the start of the following summer season. Beginning on 25 May 1924, Ukrvozdukhput ran a weekly service from Kharkov to Odessa and a twice-weekly service to Kiev. Flights ceased on 1 October for the winter season, during which time seven of the more powerful, six-seater Komet III aircraft were bought.

Flights resumed on 15 May 1925, with the addition of new routes beyond the borders of the Ukrainian SSR: Kharkov to Moscow via Kursk and Orel (420 miles) and Kharkov to Rostov-on-Don via

Artyomovsk (250 miles). The route between the Russian and Ukrainian capitals proved popular, with the state-subsidised ticket price of 34 rubles only slightly more expensive than the train fare.

A notice in the cabin gave a list of inflight safety measures for passengers to follow: after take-off, those in the window seats were to look out and check the landing gear and immediately inform the pilots – who were unable to see that part of the plane from their flight deck – if any of the wheels had fallen off; during the flight, it was forbidden to drink alcohol, to throw anything out of the aeroplane, to open the cabin door or the hatch in the toilet ceiling, to throw cigarette butts on the floor, to touch the flight-control cables that passed along the cabin ceiling or to enter the luggage compartment.

In 1925, Ukrvozdukhput carried a total of 1,550 passengers and 11.6 tons of cargo. Flights to Kiev and Odessa ceased in 1926, when it was decided that these routes, though useful to the Ukrainian SSR, served no practical military purpose. Instead, the airline began operating the service previously run by the recently defunct Junkers Luftverkehr company, flying between Moscow, Baku and Tiflis. The fleet continued to expand and in 1928 the airline became the first customer for the Kalinin K-4, built in Kharkov.

By February 1928, Ukrvozdukhput flew as far as Pahlavi in Persia (now Bandar-e Anzali, Iran), where passengers and cargo were transferred to a Junkers Luftverkehr Persia plane to fly to Tehran. From here passengers could take connecting flights to a number of other Persian cities.

In 1928, Soviet leader Joseph Stalin implemented the first five-year economic plan, with the intention of transforming the USSR from a poor agricultural state into a strong industrial nation. An important part of the development was to enable the country to produce its own aircraft. The shift to a centrally planned economy had begun and it was decided there was no further reason to sustain multiple independent airlines.

Ukrvozdukhput and Dobrolet were officially merged on 20 January 1930, retaining the Dobrolet name. A month later the Civil Aviation Council was dissolved and its functions transferred to the Main Inspectorate of the Civil Air Fleet. In November, Dobrolet was converted into a state-owned organisation and its shareholder status was abolished. The Main Inspectorate of the Civil Air Fleet and Dobrolet were merged into the newly formed All-Union Association of the Civil Air Fleet (Vsesoyuznogo Ob'yedineniya Grazhdanskogo Vozdushnogo Flota), administered by the Council of Labour and Defence of the USSR. This body was divided into eight Air Transport Directorates: Moscovian, Siberian, East Siberian, Far Eastern, Ukrainian, Transcaucasian, Central Asian and Kazakh.

Capital invested in civil aviation of the USSR. Text on the airport runway reads: **MOSCOW.** Each whole aeroplane symbol in the columns is equal to 30 million rubles. Postcard, 1932.

4. AEROFLOT

The birth of a giant

The overall volume of air passengers in the USSR was low in comparison with numbers in other industrialised countries. By the end of 1930, with a route network of 18,300 miles, the Civil Air Fleet and Deruluft had transported 12,013 and 2,396 passengers respectively – in total, 29 times less than the US and 6.5 times less than Germany. The main reason for the disparity lay in the USSR's small and out-dated fleet of around 50 aeroplanes, whose frequent technical failures meant they were rarely in regular use.

A central goal of Stalin's first five-year plan was to match and then surpass the air-traffic volumes of the advanced capitalist countries. As part of this ambitious scheme, it was imperative that domestic manufacture replace the importation of German-built Junkers and Dornier planes. Two new Soviet-produced aircraft made their first test flights in 1929: the ANT-9 (an acronym of Andrei Nikolayevich Tupolev, the plane's designer) was the first multi-engine, all-metal Soviet airliner; the single-engine Kalinin K-5 looked similar to its predecessor the K-4, but was larger and more comfortable. Production issues delayed their introduction and as a temporary measure several Junkers bombers had their military fittings removed and were transferred from the Air Force to the Civil Air Fleet.

Two-seater Polikarpov biplanes, formerly belonging to the Air Force, were used to carry mail and freight. From 1931, they also dispatched the printing plates for the Pravda newspaper to cities in the European region of the USSR. As they were required to fly in almost all weathers, only the best pilots were selected for the task. If the condition of the destination airfield was unsuitable for landing, the precious plates would be dropped by parachute.

The first ANT-9 aircraft entered service in 1931. Powered by three engines, it could carry nine passengers and three crew and was equipped with a toilet and separate luggage compartment. Though the aircraft took Soviet civil aviation to a new standard, it was heavier and had a lower carrying capacity than the latest Western airliners. In addition, there were concerns over its safety since in the event of even a single engine failure, the ANT-9 was rendered incapable of flight. Initially the ground crew were simply not equipped to service such an aircraft: it took five people around two and a half hours to refuel, a process carried out manually using buckets, with approximately 5 per cent of the fuel wasted through spillage.

The development of aviation in this country is among the main tasks of socialist construction and the defence of the USSR. Poster by D. Babichenko, 1931.

On the wings of the aircraft: **MAXIM / GORKY**. A photomontage depicting Joseph Stalin and Maxim Gorky observing the Agitation Squadron. *USSR in Construction Magazine*, No.1, 1935.

Nevertheless, in terms of passenger comfort, this was the first Soviet aircraft that was at all comparable to its Western counterparts.

The Kalinin K-5, also introduced in 1931, had space for two pilots and eight passengers, with a luggage compartment and toilet at the rear. It was simpler and cheaper than the ANT-9 in both production and operation and thus became the most popular pre-war Soviet airliner, with almost 300 built.

Another aircraft from the Tupolev Design Bureau, the gigantic ANT-14, took to the air for the first time in the same year. Powered by five engines, operated by a crew of five (two pilots, a navigator and two flight mechanics) and carrying up to 36 passengers, it was the biggest airliner in the world. If there was a problem with the engines during the flight, they could be accessed through a hatch in the central section of the fuselage. In addition, to make the flight as comfortable as possible, Tupolev had incorporated elements of train-carriage design into the passenger cabin. Ultimately, however, the size of the ANT-14 was its undoing: it proved too large for general passenger services and the factories with the capacity to manufacture it were inundated with military orders.

On 25 February 1932, all aspects of Soviet civil aviation came under the control of the Main Directorate of the Civil Air Fleet (Glavnoye Upravleniye Grazhdanskovo Vozdushnogo Flota) and exactly one month later the official title Aeroflot (meaning Air Fleet) was adopted. By the end of the year, the number of aircraft produced domestically exceeded the number imported.

A new, much improved version of the ANT-9 appeared in 1933, fitted with two Soviet M-17 engines that were both more powerful and more reliable. The majority of the original ANT-9 aircraft already in service were converted to this new standard.

In March of the same year, a new division appeared within Aeroflot: the Agitation Squadron, which had no precedent in the aeronautical world. Its main task was to support political and economic campaigns and to encourage the popularity of civil aviation. Each of the aircraft in the squadron was named after a newspaper, with the single ANT-14, as the flagship, labelled 'Pravda'.

A campaign was launched to raise funds for an even bigger flagship: the ANT-20 Maxim Gorky (named after the famous Soviet writer). Powered by eight engines, it was equipped with a cinema, photographic darkroom, printing office, internal telephone system and external loudspeakers. The aircraft was used to demonstrate the technical advances made by the Soviet Union to the rest of the world. On 19 June 1934, two days after its maiden flight, it flew over Red Square.

Tragedy occurred less than a year later, however, when on 18 May 1935 the Maxim Gorky flew over Moscow escorted by a Polikarpov I-5, a single-seater biplane fighter. While making an unauthorised loop manoeuvre, the pilot of the I-5, Nikolay Blagin, miscalculated, hitting the giant plane's right wing. Both planes crashed, killing Blagin and all 47 people on board the ANT-20.

The ANT-14 was taken out of service in 1937 after making over a thousand flights and carrying some 40,000 passengers. It was put on display in Gorky Park, Moscow, and used as a cinema.

By this time the Agitation Squadron had expanded to include 32 aircraft. Running costs were high, however, and in March 1939 the head of civil aviation announced that the squadron would be disbanded. The official pretext was that a single squadron was insufficient for the task and that the propaganda role should therefore be transferred to the entire Civil Air Fleet. In fact, however, with the Great Purge of the late 1930s in full swing, Stalin and his entourage had found a far more effective method of influence – fear of arrest, torture, imprisonment in the Gulag and execution.

With factories being pushed to reach overambitious targets set by the five-year economic plans, the volume of both aircraft and flights were rising – though the number of accidents was also increasing at an even faster rate. With inadequate resources and organisation, many pilots lacked sufficient training and were required to fly poorly maintained aircraft, without basic cockpit instruments or radios.

Throughout 1935, Aeroflot transported 96,298 passengers, 9,802 tons of freight and 4,290 tons of mail. The fleet had grown to around one thousand (mostly out-dated) aeroplanes: 47 ANT-9s, 81 Kalinin K-5s, more than 800 small Polikarpov biplanes and about 100 hundred other aircraft, both Soviet- and foreign-made. Ticket prices were high, with the result that most passengers were business travellers – making it apparent that Soviet air travel was not for the masses.

To improve the aircraft-production process, a delegation of Soviet specialists led by Tupolev made an extensive tour of factories in the US and Europe. They were able to familiarise themselves with foreign methods of aircraft manufacture and even purchased a single American Douglas DC-2. The best commercial aircraft at the time, the DC-2 was fitted with the latest navigational equipment, including an autopilot, and could carry fourteen passengers at speeds of up to 195 mph. The aircraft was thoroughly studied and tested before

Civil Aviation Moscow State Aviation and Automotive Publishing House, issue 19, October 1932. Magazine front cover featuring an ANT-14.

joining the ANT-9 fleet flying the Moscow to Prague route – Aeroflot's first incursion into Europe – which had opened on 1 September 1936.

The airline was in urgent need of more sophisticated aircraft, but meanwhile every effort was made to improve passenger comfort in existing planes. Carpets were fitted, seats were upholstered and passengers on a number of routes were able to purchase in-flight refreshments. In addition, 'high-speed' Soviet aircraft – the ANT-35 and ZiG-1 – were hurried into production. Flying at 220 mph, the ten-seater ANT-35 was capable of twice the speed of the K-5 and ANT-9. In order to attain this, cabin height was reduced, making it awkward to walk inside or use the toilet, while the passenger seating was set lower down. Nevertheless, equipped with retractable landing gear, wing flaps, autopilot, two-way radio, ventilation, lighting and heating, the aircraft was a huge improvement. Most importantly, it could continue to fly on a single engine if the other one failed.

Two ANT-35s started flying between Moscow and Stockholm in summer 1937, though the aircraft were suspended after one was forced to make an emergency landing in a field near Stockholm on 19 August 1938. In 1940, another seven entered service, with Aeroflot's Ukraine Directorate operating the Kiev to Moscow and Kiev to Odessa routes. In total, only eleven examples of this model were built.

The ZiG-1 was a twelve-seater plane designed by André Laville, a French national who worked at the Aircraft Research Institute in Moscow. He was suspended by the People's Commissariat for Internal Affairs (the NKVD) while working on the plane, but the project was continued under the direction of lead engineer A. V. Kulev. The finished aircraft was named after the factory where it was built – Zavod Imeni Goltsmana (Goltsman Plant), which itself had been named after Abram Goltsman, the first head of the Main Directorate of the Civil Air Fleet until his death in a plane crash on 5 September 1933, together with his deputy and other directors of the Soviet aviation industry.

The inaugural flight of the ZiG-1 took place in spring 1935. Initial tests were promising until a fatal crash on 27 November killed chief engineer Kulev and the four-man crew. A second prototype was built and by summer 1937 the aircraft was ready for mass production. By that time, Goltsman had posthumously fallen from grace with the Soviet political leadership and the aircraft was prosaically renamed PS-89 (Passazhirskii Samolet – passenger aircraft, from factory number 89). Flights between Moscow and Simferopol in the Crimea finally began in April 1938, but in total only eight PS-89s were ever built, including the two prototypes.

To speed up the modernisation of the Aeroflot fleet, the Soviet government acquired a licence to manufacture the new American Douglas DC-3. This latest model from the famous plane manufacturer

ФЕВРАЛЬ 1933 год

ГРАЖДАНСКАЯ АВИАЦИЯ

N 2

МОСКВА ГОСАВИААВТОИЗДАТ

Civil Aviation Moscow State Aviation Publishing House, issue 2, February 1933. Magazine front cover depicting an ANT-14 and an airship flying over an industrialised landscape with a statue of Lenin.

Aeroflot Aircraft Timetable. Depicting an ANT-35 (PS-35) flying over the Kremlin, summer 1937.

could carry 21 passengers at a cruising speed of 185 mph. Once the contract with Douglas had been signed, Soviet engineers visited the Douglas factory in Santa Monica to learn the finer technical details of the DC-3's construction. As part of the agreement, the Soviets also bought eighteen DC-3s, with the first three arriving in spring 1937 to become part of the Aeroflot fleet. The rest were divided between the Air Force and the Polar Aviation service.

Despite these promising signs, 1937 was the most difficult pre-war year for Aeroflot. Many flights were cancelled because of a shortage of fuel caused by military operations in which the USSR assisted China in its fight against Japan and the Republicans against the Nationalists in the Spanish Civil War. In addition, the rate of manufacture of civil aircraft was slow, delaying essential renewal of the fleet. The airline's only DC-2 had crashed between Prague and Moscow and most of the other aircraft were out-dated, still lacking radio and navigation equipment. But the biggest tragedy for Soviet Civil Aviation was political rather than technological.

Stalin's Great Purge of perceived counter-revolutionaries was at its height between 1936 and 1938 – and Aeroflot personnel did not

Winter Aircraft Timetable. Depicting a PS-89 equipped with skis, flying through a snowstorm, 1937-38.

escape the attention of the NKVD. By the end of 1937, 360 employees had been arrested and a further 800 fired from their jobs. In the first half of 1938, the NKVD arrested another 110 Aeroflot workers, including fifteen heads of department along with their deputies and 27 pilots. Many were sentenced to death after staged trials in which they were found guilty of sabotage, espionage or conspiracy, and chairmen of territorial directorates and even past directors of civil aviation were also executed. Aeronautical experts, among them famous aircraft designers such as Polikarpov, Kalinin, Tupolev, Putilov, Neman, Bartini, Myasischev and Petlyakov, were also arrested. The founders of Soviet rocketry were badly affected too, with leaders in the field including Korolev and Glushko imprisoned.

Andrei Tupolev was detained from 21 October 1937 until his eventual release in July 1941, days after the outbreak of the Great Patriotic War (World War II). In February 1939, he was moved from his prison to a 'sharashka' (prison design bureau) in the Moscow suburbs, where together with other incarcerated specialists he developed new military aircraft. The planes carrying his ANT initials were renamed, so the ANT-9 became the PS-9, ANT-35 became

In the late 1930s, most of the Aeroflot fleet consisted of small biplanes like this Polikarpov R-5. The route from Stalinabad (now Dushanbe), the capital of the Tajik SSR, over the Pamir mountains to Khorog (pictured here, 1937) is still considered one of the world's most dangerous air routes.

PS-35, and so on. The punishment of designer Konstantin Kalinin was more severe: accused of anti-Soviet activities and espionage (the standard allegation in 1937–38), he was executed in Voronezh on 22 April 1938.

Between 1933 and 1937, the period of the second five-year plan, passenger traffic increased more than five-fold and freight 27-fold. In regions with few or no roads or railways, targets for passenger air transport were exceeded, while where alternative means of transport were available, they were not reached. The lack of a reliably regular service and the fact that those flights that ran often used converted Air Force bombers with poor passenger facilities were among the main reasons for the low uptake. In addition, with an average airspeed of around 110 mph, flights such as those from Moscow to Tbilisi or Moscow to Tashkent were tedious in the extreme, typically taking more than a day to complete. The emphasis for the next five-year plan, from 1938 to 1942, would be not growth, but improved safety, regularity and facilities.

By 1 November 1938, in the Moscow suburb of Khimki, factory 84 had completed assembly of the first DC-3 using parts purchased from the US. Within a year, six Soviet DC-3 aeroplanes, newly designated PS-84 (passenger aircraft built at factory 84), were

left: French magazine advertisement. A twin-engine ANT-9 flies over a map of the Soviet Union showing the main air routes. *Revue de Moscou*, No.2, 1936.

right: French magazine advertisement. An ANT-35 flies over the Dnieper Hydroelectric Station in Zaporizhia, Ukrainian SSR. *Revue de Moscou*, No.4, 1937.

constructed. Eighteen Soviet specialists had been trained at the Douglas factory in the US, and under the supervision of V. M. Myasishchev the engineering drawings had all been converted from imperial to metric, in line with Soviet standards. The design was also adapted to accommodate Soviet engines and cockpit instruments and changes were made to the landing gear and cabin layout. Once official tests ended in December 1939, the PS-84 entered service, becoming Aeroflot's main aircraft. Soon afterwards, Myasishchev was arrested as part of the purges, leaving production to be overseen by designer A. A. Senkov and chief engineer B. P. Lisunov.

Six months earlier, on 5 May 1939, 20-year-old Muscovite Elsa Gorodetskaya had been appointed as Aeroflot's first air stewardess. She was officially hired as a storekeeper, as this new role had not yet been given its own designation. Only women shorter than 5 feet 4 inches and weighing no more than 8 stone 3 lbs were accepted for the job, the height restriction enabling them to move around the cabin with ease and their low weight having little impact on the overall payload. About two hours before departure, Gorodetskaya arrived at Moscow's Frunze airfield carrying a heavy suitcase filled with cutlery, plates, glasses and thermos flasks of boiling water from the airport restaurant. She cleaned the cabin and prepared snacks,

left: *Civil Aviation*, issue 3, March 1939. Magazine front cover depicting Joseph Stalin, marking the 18th Congress of the Russian Communist Party (Bolsheviks) held from 10 - 21 March 1939 in Moscow.

right: *Science and Technology*, August 1938. Magazine front cover: the flag of the Civil Air Fleet flies above the Kremlin; above this a PS-89 speeds past.

and then, after take-off, introduced herself and the flight crew to the passengers. Her inaugural flight was from Moscow to Ashgabat (in the Turkmen SSR), with two intermediate stops at Stalingrad (now Volgograd) and Baku. Thirteen hours after leaving Moscow, the plane landed in the capital of the Turkmen SSR. For passengers, this was greatly preferable to a train ride of 129 hours 30 minutes.

Flights between Moscow and Berlin were resumed on 21 January 1940, almost three years after the liquidation of Deruluft. This was made possible by the signing of the 1939 Molotov–Ribbentrop Pact agreeing to non-aggression between Germany and the USSR. Thanks largely to the success of the PS-84, the volume of passenger traffic in the first half of 1941, before the USSR entered World War II, increased 150 per cent over the same period in 1940, bringing the total to 225,023. At the outbreak of the war, Aeroflot was flourishing: the PS-84 was being produced at a rate of around one per day; support equipment was rapidly improving; and the installation of navigational aids both on the ground and in the aircraft would soon allow Aeroflot to enter the international arena. However, the approaching war was to have a dramatic effect on the airline.

Aeroflot USSR Air Route Moscow – Ashgabat in 13 hours. The Moscow - Ashgabat route is flown by the comfortable and fast 21-seat passenger aircraft PS-84. Ticket price 360 rubles.

Although the advert says 'PS-84', the route was actually flown by original DC-3s, as pictured, since the PS-84 was not yet in service. *Illustrated Newspaper*, a publication by the *Pravda* newspaper, 16 June 1939.

5. WAR!

Everything for the front, everything for victory!

At dawn on 22 June 1941, Germany, with the support of Italy and Romania, launched Operation Barbarossa, invading the USSR and breaking the Molotov–Ribbentrop Pact. Civil air routes in the European region of the USSR were immediately suspended. The following day, Aeroflot's operations were subordinated to the People's Commissariat of Defence in order to form special air groups to support the Red Army. Many civil flight and technical schools were also put under Air Force control.

At that time, Aeroflot had some 2,000 aircraft: about 80 PS-84s and DC-3s, with the majority of the fleet consisting of small, two-seater Polikarpov biplanes. The Aeroflot workforce was inducted into military service, with many of its pilots, navigators, technicians, radio operators and other experts joining long-range bomber units. On 29 July 1941, after the first month of war, a report was delivered to Stalin detailing the current operational capacity of the Soviet Air Force. A total of 755 Aeroflot aircraft had been transferred to special air groups, though of these, 85 had already been lost: 63 to enemy action (both in the air and on the ground), seven to friendly fire and fifteen through accidental damage. In an attempt to improve these statistics, a number of planes were camouflaged or fitted with machine guns, though losses continued at an alarming rate and by the end of August a total of 410 planes had been destroyed through enemy action alone, including 32 PS-84s.

As the war progressed, many aircraft plant and repair facilities were forced to relocate to the East. In October and November, machinery and personnel at the PS-84 production plant were moved from Khimki (in Moscow) to Tashkent (in the Uzbek SSR). Production restarted in January 1942 under the direction of lead engineer B. P. Lisunov and the aircraft was renamed Li-2 to reflect this. To speed up manufacture, the quality of materials used for various parts was reduced so that by the end of 1942, 386 Li-2s had been built.

The special air groups of the Civil Air Fleet were tasked with the transportation of military personnel, medical supplies, arms, ammunition and other freight to the front and evacuating the wounded on their return flights. Others flew reconnaissance missions and others still dropped propaganda leaflets behind enemy lines. To reduce losses, the number of night flights was increased and camouflaged airfields were used, lit only by torches or moonlight.

Youth, get on [board] planes. Poster by artist G. Klutsis, 1934.

In the winter of 1941–42, the role of the special air groups expanded to include offensive missions: PS-84s were used to transport paratroopers, partisans and agents into enemy territory and Polikarpov biplanes dropped incendiary fire bags and, later, conventional bombs. That such slow aircraft were used as bombers demonstrates how desperate the Soviet situation had become during this period of the war, yet by flying close to the ground, the biplanes were often able to outmanoeuvre the faster German Messerschmitt fighters. As greater numbers of Li-2 planes received defensive armament, they also began to be used as long-range night bombers. As pilots gained more experience, the level of losses decreased sharply: in 1941, one loss was sustained for every 324 sorties, while in 1942 this was reduced to one in every 840 sorties.

Through the entire period of the Great Patriotic War (1941–45), the Soviets produced an estimated 112,000 combat aircraft. They received another 18,700 from the US and Great Britain under the Lend–Lease agreement, which allowed the US government to supply military equipment to countries whose defence was vital to the security of the country. Lend–Lease planes were delivered by several routes, including 8,000 flown by Soviet pilots from Ladd airfield near Fairbanks, Alaska, to the city of Krasnoyarsk in Siberia. In winter 1941, a new route was devised over the largely unknown, uninhabited and unforgiving terrain of Eastern Siberia. Some fifteen primary and ancillary airfields were constructed from scratch or rebuilt from existing facilities, spread across more than 3,700 miles of territory: from Uelkal on the Chukotka coast to Seymchan; over the Chersky mountain range to Oymyakon; and across the Verkhoyansk range to Yakutsk, Kirensk and Krasnoyarsk.

Air expeditions were organised to search for suitable locations for airfields. Once these were identified, workers, construction materials and equipment were transported to the sites by plane, steamer and reindeer sled. Construction teams lived in dugouts, confronting temperatures as low as minus 45°C, fierce winds, snowstorms and, during the spring thaw, impassable mud. Despite these conditions, the airfields were ready by summer, and airborne ferry operations were soon able to start.

As well as many fighters and bombers, between October 1942 and September 1945, the Soviets ferried a total of 707 C-47s along the Krasnoyarsk route. These were American-built military transport DC-3 aircraft that were more reliable and outperformed the Li-2s, with more powerful engines, improved radio and navigation equipment and better overall construction. From spring 1943, they also started to enter the Civil Air Fleet. (At the end of November 1943, Stalin flew to the Tehran Conference in Iran on board a Lend–

Glory to the Heroes of the Great Patriotic War! Glory to the Stalinist Falcons! Poster by artists L. Torich and P. Vandyshev, from the beginning of the Great Patriotic War (World War II), 1941.

Lease Douglas C-47 rather than a specially prepared Li-2.)

In the East, a limited number of civil air routes remained active throughout the war, mostly in areas where aircraft were the only transport option. Some international routes, including Tashkent to Kabul (in Afghanistan), Alma-Ata to Hami (in China) and Ulan-Ude in Eastern Siberia to Ulaanbaatar (in Mongolia), continued to operate. A Moscow to Tehran route opened in June 1942 and, at the request of the Iranian government, internal flights by Aeroflot from Tehran to Mashhad, Tabriz and Pahlavi were launched in April 1944.

As territory initially taken by the invading German troops was regained, captured German Junkers Ju-52s (the standard Luftwaffe transport aircraft) were repaired and added to the civil fleet. The tide of the war had turned in the Soviets' favour, and increasing numbers of regular air routes west of Moscow were authorised to resume. However, as they retreated, German troops often destroyed airport infrastructure, necessitating significant efforts of reconstruction.

The German Instrument of Surrender, which was the official document recording the end of Nazi Germany, was signed after midnight (Moscow time) in Berlin on 8 May. On 9 May, Alexei Ivanovich Semenkov, commander of the 2nd Sevastopol Aviation Regiment, landed at Moscow's Vnukovo aerodrome carrying the document. This date, designated Victory Day, continues to be celebrated in Russia every year.

Over the course of the war, the Civil Air Fleet transported a total of almost 2.36 million passengers and 278,000 tons of cargo. This included some 1.6 million soldiers and officers, of whom 350,000 were wounded, as well as 26,000 tons of ammunition and more than 2,000 tons of preserved blood. Just over a thousand civil aircraft were lost in combat, both in the air and on the ground, almost 80 per cent of these between 1941 and 1942.

Aeroflot personnel and aircraft had proved essential to the Soviet war effort, playing a vital role in every major engagement including the Leningrad Air Bridge; the defence of Moscow, Sevastopol and the Caucasus; the Battles of Stalingrad and Kursk; the liberation of the Western USSR; and the Battle of Berlin. In all, 15,000 crew received medals and orders, with fifteen Aeroflot pilots being awarded the ultimate honour of Hero of the Soviet Union. A total of 816 personnel were killed, of whom 445 were pilots.

On the ground and above the ground we will burn the enemy down! Poster by artists P. Sokolov-Skalya and A. Druzhkov, 1941.

6. RECONSTRUCTION

The decade following the war

The war had devastated the Western territories of the USSR, but with his fourth and fifth five-year economic plans, Joseph Stalin was determined to establish the country as a leading industrial power – and Aeroflot was to play an important role in this undertaking. With the larger civil airports yet to be repaired after the war, the airline had to make use of military airfields. Intent on increasing capacity, however, by 1945 it had already carried 537,000 passengers, far exceeding the figure of 359,000 in 1940, the last fully operational year before the war.

By late 1946, the Aeroflot fleet consisted of more than 3,100 planes, of which the vast majority – 2,500 – were small Polikarpov Po-2 biplanes. Alongside these, forming the backbone of the fleet, were 250 Li-2 aircraft and a similar number of Lend–Lease C-47 planes. In addition, there were 45 seaplanes, including six Lend–Lease Catalinas and 39 Shavrov Sh-2s. About 40 aircraft seized from Germany (mainly Ju-52 and Siebel-204 models) were also pressed into service.

One problem with this assortment of aircraft was that most of the Li-2 and C-47 planes had been designed for transporting cargo rather than passengers, a problem that was addressed in the years immediately following the war by retrofitting them with modified passenger cabins. Over time, the lack of spare engines for the C-47s also became an issue: from 1947, several were refitted with Soviet ASh-62IR engines and redesignated as TS-62s. In 1948, two C-47s received the much more powerful ASh-82FN engines: designated TS-82, they performed well in the heat and high altitude of the hazardous route between Stalinabad (now Dushanbe) and Khorog in the Tajik SSR.

Even under such conditions, the benefit of air travel was obvious. An extreme example of time-saving was recorded on the route between the Kazakh SSR capital Alma-Ata and Balkhash. Aeroflot Li-2 aircraft flew the 260 miles in two hours, while the same journey by train took 157 hours – almost a whole week. In the absence of a direct rail link between the cities, the train had to travel north all the way to Novosibirsk in south-western Siberia before returning south, covering a total distance of 2,354 miles – almost ten times the length of the direct flight. A train ticket cost between 203 and 610 rubles, depending on the class, while the price for an air ticket was 390 rubles for a 'hard' seat and 430 for a 'soft' seat.

Save Time! Use Air Transport.

5 May, opening of Summer navigation. All capitals of the Union's republics, big cities, resorts of Crimea, and Caucasus are connected by air transport. Buy airplane tickets in the Aeroflot city agencies.

Advertisement in weekly magazine *Ogonëk*, depicting an Ilyushin 12, the first post-WWII Soviet airliner, April 1949.

All information at the city agencies and airports of the Civil Air Fleet.
Timetable leaflet, artist S. Sakharov, c.1948

This dual pricing structure, which survived into the late 1950s, was a legacy of the war years. Demilitarised Li-2 aircraft, alongside TS-62s and post-war Li-2Ts, lacked basic comforts such as cabin lining, insulation, heating, luggage racks and sometimes even a toilet. Passengers faced each other on folding wooden seats attached to the fuselage, instead of the standard, more comfortable, aircraft seating familiar today. If a 'soft-seat' aeroplane was used, passengers would expect to pay a 10 per cent supplement at the airport.

Production of the Li-2 was discontinued in 1954, by which time a total of 4,960 of these Soviet Dakotas had been built, including 742 of the passenger model. Simultaneously, the last, decrepit TS-62s were being phased out of the Aeroflot fleet.

During the war, aircraft designer Sergei Ilyushin had found fame with his successful Il-2 assault plane, nicknamed the 'flying tank'. In late 1943, as the Soviets gained the upper hand in the conflict, he began work on what was to become the first post-war Soviet transport plane, the Ilyushin Il-12. Introduced on passenger routes in summer 1947, the Il-12 had a standard cabin for 27 passengers and, with a cruising speed of 210 mph, was 60 mph faster than the Li-2.

Despite these advantages, the Il-12's first years of service were plagued with technical problems. Its engines proved unreliable, requiring replacement after only 150 flight hours, and in 1949 it was deemed unsafe for the payload to exceed eighteen passengers,

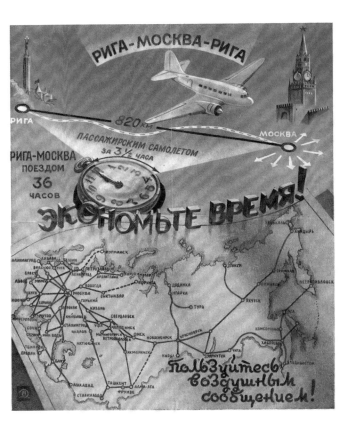

Riga – Moscow – Riga. SAVE TIME! Use Air Transport! Riga – Moscow, 820 km. By train 36 hours. By passenger airplane in 3 ½ hours. Promotional brochure, c.1950.

rendering it uneconomical to run. Production at the Khodynka factory in Moscow – which had already manufactured 663 units – ceased that same year. Most of the technical issues were resolved in the early 1950s, including the introduction of a revised cabin lay-out accommodating 21 passengers on standard flights and up to 32 on popular short routes.

In one notorious event in June 1954, flight engineer V. Polyakov, who had learned how to pilot twin-engine aircraft during the war, hijacked an empty Il-12 from Novosibirsk airport. Accusing his wife of infidelity, he threatened to commit suicide by crashing the aircraft into his own house. For several hours, the 'Siberian Othello', as he was later nicknamed, circled low over the city, veering sharply to avoid buildings and causing great commotion on the ground.

SOVIET UNION ☭

No. 12 (82)   DECEMBER 1956

Caption inside reads: **High above the Pamirs at an altitude of 16,500 feet, passengers have oxygen at their disposal. Pictured is Davlyat Khudododoyeva, member of the Khorog Dance Ensemble, on her way to a concert in Stalinabad.** Photograph by V. Ruikovich, *Soviet Union Illustrated Monthly*, December 1956.

Attempts to talk Polyakov into landing were unsuccessful, so two fighter jets were scrambled to force the Il-12 away from the city and shoot it down. Eventually, Polyakov landed safely with no damage to the plane. Severe punishment awaited him, but Ilyushin made a personal appeal on his behalf, claiming he had proved the Il-12's safe handling under extreme conditions. As a consequence, Polyakov was sentenced to a relatively lenient three years in prison.

In 1947, both the Ilyushin and the Tupolev Design Bureaus started testing bigger and more ambitious prototypes with four-piston engines and between 60 and 70 passenger seats: the Il-18 and Tu-70. While they performed well, they proved too large and complicated for airfields that were often little more than rough landing strips with wooden huts for passenger terminals and no infrastructure to service and maintain large aircraft.

In 1946, the Soviet government ordered the construction of a new agricultural aircraft to replace the lightweight Po-2 biplanes. At factory 153 in Novosibirsk, the newly formed Antonov Design Bureau built a large, single-engine biplane that later became known

top: Aeroflot SSSR / Moscow – Khabarovsk.

bottom: **Aeroflot SSSR / Moscow – Kazan – Sverdlovsk – Omsk – Novosibirsk – Krasnoyarsk – Irkutsk – Chita – Khabarovsk.** Leaflet, 1950. Aeroflot's three longest flights began from Moscow-Vnukovo to Khabarovsk (4,295 miles) in the Soviet Far East. Il-12 aircraft made eight intermediate landings: Kazan, Sverdlovsk, Omsk, Novosibirsk, Krasnoyarsk, Irkutsk, Chita and Tygda (not shown above). Depending on the schedule, the journey took 32 hours 55 minutes or 42 hours 10 minutes (with an overnight stay in Krasnoyarsk) with 21 hours 55 minutes in the air. From Khabarovsk, flights No.1 and No.11 continued to their respective final destinations. No.1 flew to Vladivostok (4,680 miles) with overnight stops in Novosibirsk and Chita; the journey from Moscow lasted 56 hours 5 minutes. No.11 reached Yuzhno-Sakhalinsk (4,750 miles) on Sakhalin Island after 57 hours 45 minutes, including nine stopovers (overnight stays in Krasnoyarsk and Tygda) and 24 hours 20 minutes of flight time.

as the Antonov An-2. Although it already looked obsolete when it made its first flight on 31 August 1947, state approval was granted and in 1949 production started in Kiev.

Instead of flying its first missions over the Ukrainian steppe, the An-2 received its baptism in the Arctic. It had all the advantages required for polar aviation: a powerful engine, good cockpit visibility and a spacious cargo compartment. Most importantly, it could land on, and take off from, ice floes in the severest of conditions. Given

top left: Passengers board an Il-12P at Moscow's Vnukovo airport, 1956.

bottom left: A Polikarpov biplane crop spraying, 1950s.

top: **AN-2**. Double-folded postcard commemorating the 30th anniversary of the first Antonov An-2 flight, 31 August 1977.

bottom: Aeroflot sales brochure presenting the Antonov An-2, 1960s.

the nickname Annushka, the unpretentious biplane became popular with geologists, foresters, firefighters, fishermen and paratroopers.

Because of its originally intended role in agriculture, the An-2 also became known by the name of its predecessor, the Po-2 'Kukuruznik' (corn-crop duster). In addition to its initial use spraying fields with fertiliser, it was quickly employed for a range of similar farming tasks including sowing crops, spraying pesticides, defoliation of cotton plants prior to harvest and chemical desiccation of sunflowers and rice. A grass strip or small field was all it needed for take off and landing, and its wheels could be replaced by skis or floats as required.

By the early 1960s, the aircraft had become indispensable to a large section of the Soviet population. Small airfields had proliferated, and the twelve-seater An-2 was perfectly suited to connect regional centres with remote villages tucked away among woods and hills. People much preferred an uncomfortable 30-minute flight in a noisy cabin to a tedious and bumpy six-hour bus ride. Workers, businessmen, collectivised farmers, housewives, schoolchildren, grandparents – along with chickens, piglets and goats – all flew 'Annushka'. By 1962, Aeroflot had sold 25 million An-2 passenger tickets; by 1967, 100 million; and by 1977, 280 million. Over the thirty years since its introduction, this flying tractor had become an essential element within the Aeroflot fleet.

eft: An Il-14 at Dushanbe airport. Postcard, 1967.

above: Buy air tickets with home delivery.
f you wish to order a plane ticket with delivery to your home or to your place of
work, please call B 9-55-78. Orders accepted at least three days prior to departure.
Back cover advertisement from *Construction and Architecture* magazine, 1964.

Aviation in Agriculture, Aviareklama brochure, 1975.
In 1960, the Aeroflot Advertising and Information Bureau was established. This formed the basis of Aviareklama, the Central Advertising and Information Agency, created two years later. Here, professional designers oversaw the production and printing of millions of booklets, posters, calendars and brochures which were distributed to all Aeroflot destination countries.

Though rarely depicted in Aeroflot advertising, the An-2 became a legend in its own time, not only in the Soviet Union but across the world of aviation. Large-scale production continued for more than 50 years, with some 17,000 built in the USSR, Poland and China.

The light Yakovlev Yak-12 utility aircraft entered Aeroflot service in 1950, replacing the outdated Polikarpov Po-2 in the role of air taxi as well as undertaking other essential tasks including air ambulance, agricultural work and pilot training.

Little was done to modernise or improve the Civil Air Fleet until after Stalin's death in 1953. Despite his zeal for military aviation, Stalin was afraid of flying: he travelled almost exclusively by train and left the country only twice during his three decades in office. In the 1920s and 1930s, several prominent government figures had died in air crashes, which only served to intensify his fear. Stalin, whose larger objective was always the expansion of the Soviet empire, regarded civil aviation as a means to develop remote areas of the USSR rather than as a useful mode of transport for ordinary citizens.

The last civil aircraft developed under his administration was the Ilyushin Il-14, successor to the Il-12. Liked by crews because of its reliability and ease of servicing, this short-range, twin-engine airliner

Yak-12A Aeroflot. Leaflet presenting the Yak-12A at the VDNKh (Exhibition of Achievements of National Economy in Moscow), 1960.

first flew on 1 October 1950 and was introduced into Aeroflot's network on 30 November 1954, flying the route from Vnukovo airport in Moscow to Tbilisi. Between 1954 and 1960, a total of 1,348 Il-14s were built in several variants at factories across the Eastern Bloc: 687 in Moscow, 378 in Tashkent, 80 in Dresden in the GDR and 203 in Letňany, a suburb of Prague. Although Aeroflot removed its last Il-14 from regular passenger service in 1973, the aircraft was used for another two decades for tasks in support of the national economy including polar exploration to develop Soviet Arctic and Antarctic stations.

The death of Stalin and the election of Nikita Khrushchev as the new First Secretary ushered in a new age. Unlike Stalin, Khrushchev was willing to travel abroad and communicate directly with his Western counterparts. In summer 1955, he arrived at the Geneva Summit in an Il-14 and was dismayed to see his plane overshadowed by President Dwight D. Eisenhower's sleek, four-engine Lockheed Super Constellation.

Khrushchev was well aware of the advances that had been made by the West in passenger jet and turboprop aircraft design. The British had developed the De Havilland Comet, which began commercial flights in May 1952, while both the Americans and the French had similar projects under way. Following Khrushchev's promise that the USSR would 'catch up and overtake America', the Soviets could hardly allow themselves to lag behind now: they needed to build their own, suitably prestigious, passenger aircraft.

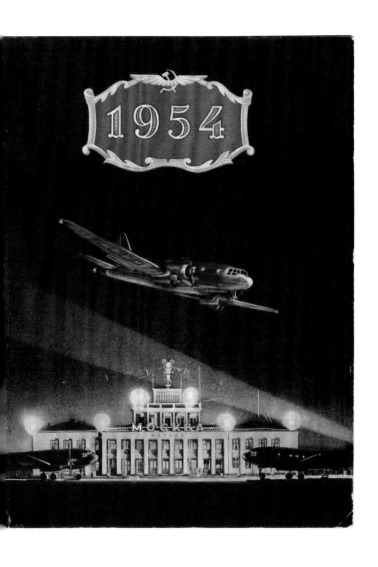

left: **Aircraft Timetable, Summer 1960** (in Russian and Estonian). This leaflet depicts the Tallinn skyline as seen from its beach, with an Ilyushin Il-14 flying overhead.

above: **1954 Moscow**. Aeroflot calendar for 1954 with an image of Vnukovo airport terminal and three Ilyushin Il-12 aircraft at night.

overleaf: **Aeroflot 11/1962** *Civil Aviation*, *Under the Aeroflot Emblem*, by artist A. Kirillova. Magazine cover, November 1962.

 АЭРОФЛО

11

962

Гражданская АВИАЦИЯ

7. ENTERING THE JET AGE

Planes for the people

Even before Stalin's death, the aircraft designer Andrei Tupolev had suggested developing a passenger airliner based on his Tu-16, a strategic jet bomber that had first flown in 1952 and was already in mass production. Adapting the design of a successful bomber rather than starting from scratch would save considerable amounts of both time and money.

As the engineers and designers at the Tupolev Bureau were taking the Tu-16 back to the drawing board, disaster struck for their British counterparts. On 2 May 1953, shortly after taking off from Calcutta (Kolkata), a BOAC (British Overseas Airways Corporation) De Havilland Comet jetliner crashed, killing its 43 passengers and crew. The aircraft had encountered adverse weather conditions, causing it to become over-stressed and break apart. The accident led to several design and operating changes, but these did not prevent a further disaster on 10 January 1954, when another BOAC Comet crashed into the Mediterranean after taking off from Rome, killing all 35 people on board. All Comet aircraft were grounded and an exhaustive investigation was launched. When no definitive cause for the crashes could be established, political and financial pressures led to the resumption of Comet flights on 23 March. But just two weeks later, on 8 April, a third Comet went down in the Mediterranean, again killing all on board. The jet's airworthiness certificate was immediately revoked, forcing all commercial operations to cease. The investigation into the last two crashes revealed that the pressurisation cycles of the cabin had caused metal fatigue at the weak points inherent in square windows, leading to catastrophic failure and explosive decompression.

That same year, Aeroflot began to use demilitarised jet bombers – four Il-28s (designated Il-20s) and three Tu-16s – for flight-crew conversion training (from piston- to jet-propelled engines) as well as for delivering urgent mail and time-sensitive newspaper printing plates.

In the meantime, construction of the first Tu-104 was completed in record time and on 17 June 1955, its inaugural flight was launched from Moscow's Zhukovsky airport (named after Nikolay Zhukovsky, regarded as the father of Russian aviation), after which it underwent a rigorous programme of tests.

Ogonëk magazine cover, May 1959. Flight attendants disembark from a Tu-104 flight at Vnukovo airport, Moscow. At the time, Aeroflot flew to around 20 capitals from Moscow.

top: Passengers in the cabin of a Tu-104, c.1956.

bottom: The serving hatch of the Tu-104 kitchen, c.1956.

top: **AEROFLOT**. *Ogonëk* magazine back cover, May 1957.

bottom: Press photographers capture the first arrival of a Tu-104A at Amsterdam, 7 July 1958.

АЭРОФЛОТ

The first passenger jet: Tu-104

On 22 March 1956, the Soviets surprised the aviation world when their first passenger jetliner landed at London Heathrow on its maiden international flight. On board were Soviet diplomats and the head of the KGB, arriving in the UK to prepare for the impending state visit of Soviet leaders Nikita Khrushchev and Nikolay Bulganin (Premier of the Soviet Union under Khrushchev). The arrival of the Tu-104 was a sensation, as if a UFO had landed on British soil. The British aviation community and the public responded with high praise and experts were astonished by the giant leap forward Soviet civil aviation had made. Though this first plane returned to the USSR three days later, it and other Tu-104s came and went throughout the landmark diplomatic mission, fulfilling various roles including delivering G. M. Malenkov and his delegation of power engineers to London.

Khrushchev had initially intended to arrive in the UK in a Tu-104 but was persuaded not to as there were still tests to run, so he and Bulganin travelled by sea, aboard the navy cruiser Ordzhonikidze arriving on 18 April. Meanwhile, since no two Tu-104s had been seen at the same time, rumours circulated in the British media that the Soviets had only one jet and were simply painting different numbers on the same plane between flights. The next day, however, all three brand-new Aeroflot Tu-104 aircraft arrived at Heathrow and stood

left: **Aeroflot**. Postcard depicting the Tu-104, c.1960

top: Bilingual Russian-English sales brochure for the Tu-104B of which 94 were built in Kazan. The larger version shown here had up to 115 seats, c.1958.

bottom: **Tu-110**. This aircraft was a Tu-104 modified to have four engines (like most Western jetliners) and intended for export. Only four were built and it never entered Aeroflot service. Leaflet, Brussels World's Fair, Soviet pavilion, 1958.

together defiantly, disproving the rumours and demonstrating the extent of the Soviet technological advance.

On 15 September 1956, Aeroflot introduced the 50-seater Tu-104 into its fleet, flying the route between Moscow, Omsk and Irkutsk three times a week. Less than a month later, the airline opened its first international jet route between Moscow Vnukovo airport and Prague, flying four times weekly. Peking (Beijing) followed in December 1956, and Rome, Paris, East Berlin, Amsterdam, Brussels, Delhi and Cairo in 1958, the year the Tupolev was awarded a gold medal at the Brussel's World Fair. For two years, the Tu-104 was the world's only commercial passenger jet plane in service. Finally, on 4 October 1958, Britain's new Comet IV was launched, followed by America's Boeing 707 on 26 October and six months later by the French Sud Aviation SE 210 Caravelle.

With the introduction of the Tu-104, the Soviets had gone almost overnight from a fleet of small, slow, uncomfortable piston-driven planes to operating jet airliners capable of reducing travel times by at least 50 per cent. However, the number of domestic Tu-104 destinations could grow only slowly as the aircraft required a long concrete runway for take-off and landing and many Soviet runways were still short and unpaved. By the end of 1960, a total of 201 Tu-104s had rolled off the production lines in Kharkov, Omsk and Kazan, almost all of them for Aeroflot, with a handful sent to the Soviet Air

АЭРОФЛОТ

АЭРОФЛОТ СССР

СССР

РАСПИСАНИЕ

ДВИЖЕНИЯ САМОЛЕТОВ

ЭСТОНСКОЙ ОТДЕЛЬНОЙ АВИАГРУППЫ
ГРАЖДАНСКОЙ АВИАЦИИ

С 15 НОЯБРЯ 1964 г. ПО 15 МАЯ 1965 г.

eft: Aeroflot brochure depicting aTu-104A, c.1960.

above: **Aircraft Timetable**. A Tu-104 on the cover of the Estonian Directorate
timetable, winter 1964-65.

Force. The only export customer was CSA Czechoslovak Airlines, which operated six Tu-104A models.

The Tu-104 was not the easiest plane to pilot: it was vulnerable to stalling and had a high landing speed. In the early 1960s, a popular rhyme to the tune of a funeral march ran: 'The Tu-104 is the fastest plane: it will get you to your grave in just two minutes'. At the time, accidents were common for all types of aircraft, and the Tu-104 was no exception.

Following a fatal accident in Moscow on 17 March 1979, the Soviet Ministry of Civil Aviation ordered the phasing out of the jet, and before the year's end Aeroflot had retired its last Tu-104. After more than 23 years of service, carrying 100 million passengers, the era of the first Soviet jet airliner was over.

Turboprops: An-10, Il-18 and Tu-114

While the Tu-104 significantly reduced travel times, its two Mikulin AM-3M turbojet engines burned an average of 14,440 lbs of fuel per hour, limiting its flight range. In April 1953, BEA (British European Airways) successfully introduced the Vickers Viscount, the first airliner driven by four, more efficient turboprop engines. Simultaneously, the Antonov, Ilyushin and Tupolev Bureaus were developing their own turboprop passenger planes for the Soviet Union.

In 1954, with World War II still fresh in the memory and the Cold War underway, Oleg K. Antonov began work on the design of two

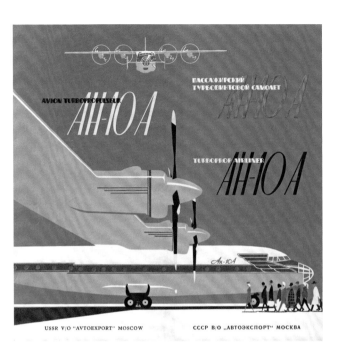

USSR V/O "AVTOEXPORT" MOSCOW　　　　СССР В/О „АВТОЭКСПОРТ" МОСКВА

Left: **Aeroflot**. Postcard depicting the Ilushin Il-18, c.1960.

top: Brochure for the An-10A turboprop airliner published by Avtoexport, c.1960.

bottom: **Ilyushin Il-18 Aircraft**. Presentation brochure from the Brussels World's Fair, Soviet pavilion, 1958.

above: **Turboprop passenger aircraft An-10A**. Aviaexport brochure, c.1962.

right: Aeroflot brochures depicting an AN-10A (top) and Il-18 (bottom), early 1960s.

near-identical aircraft – a twin-turboprop passenger liner and a military transport plane – with the idea that either could be transformed into the other as and when necessary without incurring substantial costs in time or money. The passenger version was cancelled in 1955 and only the military variant, designated An-8, was built. However, it was decided to use the same notion of interchangeability for the design of a new, heavier, four-engine aircraft. The result was the An-10, intended to accommodate 85 passengers, and the An-12, built for cargo. Both aircraft were capable of taking off and landing on unpaved runways, which was a big advantage in the USSR.

Chief aircraft engineer Sergei Ilyushin was highly critical of the dual-design concept, however, comparing the Antonov to a duck which 'can fly, swim and walk, but excels at none of them'. His bureau was developing the Il-18 purely for passenger use, without the military-style 'glass nose' needed for navigation and bombing over hostile

above: **Il-18 Turboprop passenger aircraft**. Brochure for the Ilyushin Il-18, c.1959.

right: The Il-18D, 'D' for *Dal'niy* (long distance), had an increased flight range of 4,000 miles and became the most popular version of this type. Aviaexport brochure, c.1966.

territory. This set the Il-18 apart from the Tu-104, An-10, Tu-114, Tu-124 and Tu-134, all derived from military aircraft and retaining this feature.

Even at this early stage, Aeroflot had earmarked the An-10 for use on busy, short-to-medium routes and the Il-18 for medium- to long-distance flights. On 7 March 1957, the An-10 made its maiden flight from the Antonov Design Bureau's own airfield in Svyatoshin, Kiev. However, further test flights revealed the need for modifications, mostly concerning aerodynamic stability.

Within a month, on 4 April, the 75-seat Il-18 prototype took off from the Khodynka airfield in Moscow. The test programme ran smoothly and the airliner was ready for service two years later, with passenger flights starting on 20 April 1959. The An-10 entered passenger service three months later, on 21 July, flying from Kiev to Vnukovo airport in Moscow. The next day, the plane flew on to Simferopol, a popular destination for Soviet tourists spending their holidays in the Crimean resorts. Between them the two planes had an average fuel consumption of some 5,500 lbs per hour, making them considerably more economical than the Tu-104.

This was a time of broad optimism, exciting technological achievement and rapid social development, but the An-10's good fortune was short-lived. During the winter of 1959–60, two brand

ИЛ-18Д

ИЛ-18Д

ПАССАЖИРСКИЙ
САМОЛЕТ

PASSENGER
PLANE

В/О „АВИАЭКСПОРТ" • V/O "AVIAEXPORT" • В/О „АВИАЭКСПОРТ" • V/O "AVIAEXPORT"

new An-10s crashed in almost identical circumstances on the approach to Lvov airport in the Ukrainian SSR and as a consequence the whole fleet was grounded. Investigations revealed the need for changes to the design of the flaps and the horizontal stabiliser de-icing system on the aircraft's tail, along with a revision of pilot-operating procedures. The An-10 eventually resumed service, but not before a thorough safety-testing programme and an extensive advertising campaign and promotional film to try to regain public confidence. Never used for international service, the An-10 flew shorter, domestic routes, at which it excelled, mainly in Aeroflot's Ukraine and Komi Directorates.

The Il-18's first international route from Moscow's Sheremetyevo airport to Bucharest and on to Sofia opened on 5 January 1960. Unlike the An-10, this aircraft became a successful export, selling to other Eastern Bloc states as well as to countries including China, Cuba, Ghana and Egypt. Both airliners had a huge impact on passenger numbers and on the expansion of the Aeroflot network.

By 1972, the An-10 had become a cornerstone of the Aeroflot fleet, having transported more than 38.7 million passengers and over 1.25 million tons of cargo. However, on the morning of 18 May, disaster struck again. On its approach to Kharkov airport in the Ukranian SSR, the An-10A CCCP-11215 fell from the sky, with the loss of all 122 lives

AN-12. With 1,243 produced and several still in operation today, this cargo plane proved more successful than its passenger version, the An-10. Brochure, 1960s.

on board. When the investigation revealed the cause to be fatigue cracks in the central section, all 67 Aeroflot An-10 aircraft were grounded. After thirteen years of service, the An-10 almost entirely vanished from Soviet civil aviation, with some 25 low-hours An-10s transferred to the Air Force and other aviation-industry enterprises and many others finding a second life as bars or children's cinemas in city parks throughout the USSR. Today only one example remains, at the Central Air Force Museum in Monino on the outskirts of Moscow.

The Il-18 workhorse had a much longer career. By 1980, it had transported 235 million passengers, remaining in service with Aeroflot until the fall of the Soviet Union. Subsequently, it continued to fly with many of the newly established post-Soviet airlines and is still active today in the Russian Air Force and North Korea's Air Koryo.

Aeroflot's requirement for a large intercontinental passenger airliner was fulfilled by the Tupolev Bureau in the form of the Tu-114: as with the Tu-104, the design was derived from a military aircraft, in this case the famous Tu-95 'Bear' long-range strategic bomber, in operation with the Soviet Air Force since 1956. Powered by four Kuznetsov NK-12 turboprop engines driving eight contra-rotating propellers across a swept wing, the Tu-114 was the world's fastest turboprop plane. With seating capacity for up to 220 passengers, it was truly a giant of its time, remaining the world's largest airliner until the introduction of the Boeing 747 Jumbo Jet in 1969.

The prototype was constructed at factory 156 in Moscow, then disassembled and transported to the city's Zhukovsky airfield, where it made its first flight on 15 November 1957. In June 1959, the Tu-114 crossed the Soviet border for the first time, landing in the Albanian capital of Tirana and Budapest. Later that month, it was the highlight of both the 22nd Paris Air Show and the Soviet Industrial Exhibition in New York, where it was seen by more than 40,000 Americans.

Passenger Aeroplane Tu-144. Leaflet produced for the Brussels World's Fair, 1958.

In August, Khrushchev was invited by President Eisenhower to visit the US. The Tu-114 was still in the final stages of its test programme, but this time Khrushchev was determined to make a grand entrance and could not be persuaded to use the smaller Il-18. In case the aircraft had to ditch in the ocean, several Soviet ships were positioned along the route between Iceland and New York. On 15 September, after flying non-stop for more than twelve hours, the Tu-114 landed at Andrews Air Force Base, Washington DC. It was the first time a Soviet leader had set foot on American soil and the mighty Tu-114 was greeted with amazement by the foreign press, establishing itself as a powerful weapon in the propaganda war.

On 24 April 1961, the plane began a regular passenger service on the long-distance route between Moscow and Khabarovsk, near the Chinese border. During the nine-hour flight, this 'time machine' overtook every Trans-Siberian Express train that had left Moscow's Yaroslavsky railway station in the previous seven days.

The Tu-114 was a luxury airliner. The standard cabin layout had 170 seats: 41 in the first section, followed by 48 arranged face-to-face with tables between them. Behind the stairs to the lower deck were three seats, and beyond them, four private compartments each containing three berths, then a rear cabin with a further 54 seats. The lower deck had a crew rest, two luggage compartments and a kitchen, complete with food elevators to the main cabin. Despite the many comforts, noise levels were high, especially in seats close to the huge Kuznetsov engines.

top: The An-10 CCCP-11158 photographed shortly after landing on the unpaved runway at Simferopol airport on its maiden passenger flight, 21 July 1959.

bottom: The An-10 cabin floor was at the same level as that of its cargo twin An-12, giving a ceiling height of just over 8 feet, ideal for screening in-flight films.

top right: A new Il-18B at Sochi (Adler) airport, April 1959.

bottom right: **Il-18 new 4-engine turboprop air giant**. Announcement for the first regular Il-18 passenger flights, scheduled for 20 April 1959. Two Il-18 routes opened on that day: Moscow/Vnukovo to Sochi/Adler and Moscow/Domodedovo to Alma-Ata. *Evening Moscow* newspaper, 17 April 1959.

„ИЛ-18"
НОВЫЙ
ТУРБОВИНТОВОЙ ЧЕТЫРЕХМОТОРНЫЙ ВОЗДУШНЫЙ ГИГАНТ

С 20 апреля РЕГУЛЯРНОЕ СООБЩЕНИЕ

Москва — Адлер за 3 часа.

Вылет ежедневно в 8 час. 55 мин.

Тариф снижен — билет стоит 310 руб.

Москва — Алма-Ата за 5 часов
БЕЗ ПОСАДКИ.

Вылет по понедельникам, средам и пятницам в 9 час. 20 мин.

НА БОРТУ БЕСПЛАТНОЕ ПИТАНИЕ.

На всех самолетах каждому пассажиру предоставлено право перевоза бесплатно одного ребенка до 2 лет, а также багажа до 20 кг.

.... Скорость!

Комфорт! ....

ОТКРЫТА ПРЕДВАРИТЕЛЬНАЯ ПРОДАЖА БИЛЕТОВ:

в агентстве Аэрофлота — пл. Дзержинского, в агентстве Главмосавтотранса — пл. Революции, в здании гостиницы «Москва» (бывш. «Гранд-отель»).

Справки и заказы по тел.: Б 1-26-19, В 3-46-45 и К 4-01-87.

Washington – Moscow. Postcard depicting Khruschev's flight from Moscow to Washington aboard the Tu-114 prototype, artist V. Viktorov, 1959.

In 1960, following Cuba's nationalisation without compensation of American-owned oil refineries, the US imposed an export embargo on Cuba and made several unsuccessful attempts to remove Fidel Castro, the country's Communist leader, from power. As a result, Cuba sought assistance from the politically aligned Soviet Union in the form of an air link between the two countries. With European nations preventing Soviet aircraft travelling to Cuba from entering their airspace, flights were routed across Africa. On 10 July 1962, an Aeroflot Tu-114 made the first technical flight (in which the crew familiarised themselves with the route and operational procedures) from Moscow to Conakry in Guinea and on to the Cuban capital of Havana. Three more trips were completed via Conakry until Guinea ceded to American diplomatic pressure and refused the Soviets further assistance. The air link continued via Dakar and later Algiers, but Senegal and Algeria also soon bowed to American political influence.

The Cold War escalated to an unprecedented level in October 1962 after the US discovered Soviet ballistic-missile construction sites in Cuba, placing the weapons within striking range of America. The ensuing showdown brought the world to the brink of nuclear war. With every country now forbidding Cuban-bound Soviet planes to enter their airspace, aircraft would have had to fly the route non-

Cabin of a Tu-114. Promotional brochure, c.1960.

stop, an impossible task even for the long-range Tu-114. The solution was to fit six Tu-114s with additional fuel tanks. Although this reduced the payload to 6 tons or 60 passengers, the range was increased to more than 6,800 miles. The planes were also equipped with a periscopic sextant, allowing night-time celestial navigation over the ocean.

On 22 December 1962, the first modified Tupolev, designated Tu-114D, departed from Moscow heading north. After landing to take on board the maximum fuel load at Olenya airbase near Murmansk (one of the most westerly airstrips in the USSR), it took off for Havana. The Americans watched the flight closely, but it was only when the Tupolev passed Reykjavik that they realised the Soviets were intent on reaching the Cuban capital. Icelandic, and later Canadian, air-traffic control informed the crew that the Americans would demand they descend 5,000 feet, as there were already three 'wings' (groups of military aircraft) in that zone. When New York issued the demand, the Soviet crew refused, realising that a drop in altitude would lead to an increase in fuel consumption. Shadowed by two US Air Force jets, the Tu-114D landed safely in Havana after more than fifteen hours in the air. It was a tremendous achievement, and on 7 January 1963, Aeroflot began a scheduled service on this route.

Aeroflot. Postcard depicting the Tu-114, c.1960.

The journey placed huge demands on the resilience of the crew. Strong headwinds and geomagnetic storms rendered the on-board compass inaccurate and radio contact impossible for hours at a time, meaning pilots had to fly by night across an empty North Atlantic Ocean without weather-forecast information or navigational support from the ground. Nevertheless, Aeroflot persevered, flying the route twice weekly for a further five years until flights via Africa resumed in 1968.

Four years after the Cuban Missile Crisis, the Soviets signed an agreement with Canada, much to the displeasure of the US, and on 4 November 1966, a Tu-114 touched down at Dorval airport in Montreal, after flying non-stop from Moscow. Air Canada operated a corresponding service using Douglas DC-8 aircraft, stopping for fuel in Copenhagen.

The Tu-114 was regularly used to reach destinations including Paris, Delhi, Tokyo and Sao Paulo, but with the majority of Soviet airports still lacking a suitable runway, domestic services were limited to Khabarovsk, Alma-Ata, Tashkent and Novosibirsk. Production of the Tu-114 came to an end in 1964, after a total of 33 aircraft had been built, with Aeroflot remaining the sole operator.

Aero 45. Promotional brochures, 1950s.

On 2 December 1976, CCCP-76485 made the last commercial Tu-114 flight, returning from Khabarovsk to Moscow's Domodedovo airport, the same route first flown almost sixteen years earlier. In total, the giant Tupolev flew 350,000 hours in Aeroflot's service, transporting more than 6 million passengers. Three Tu-114 aircraft remain in existence today: one at the Krivoy Rog Aviation College in Ukraine; one at the Ulyanovsk Aircraft Museum in Russia; and the prototype at the Central Air Force Museum in Monino, Moscow Oblast.

Air taxis from Czechoslovakia

On-demand air-taxi services were started in 1958 using small Czechoslovakian aircraft – the Aero 45S, Aero 145 and LET L-200 Morava. Also flying regular services, they carried up to four passengers to villages, regional centres, cities and resorts as far as 300 miles away.

Between 1958 and 1960, Aeroflot acquired some 250 Aero aeroplanes. However, they proved vulnerable on unpaved airfields, and after the production of spare parts was discontinued, they were withdrawn prematurely from service in 1965. The 180 Morava aircraft had a longer career, remaining in use until the mid-1970s.

Photograph from a promotional calendar showing a Tu-104B (CCCP-42493) from Aeroflot's International Directorate parked in front of the Ryumka terminal building, Sheremetyevo airport, Moscow, 1967.

Domestic success: Tu-124 and An-24

Another two new aircraft were introduced in October 1962: the short-to medium-range Tupolev Tu-124 and the Antonov An-24. Both began to replace the smaller Li-2s, Il-12s and Il-14s on busier routes.

With the appearance of a scaled-down Tu-104, the Tu-124 was powered by two, more efficient turbofan engines. Its original seating capacity of 44 passengers was later increased to 56. On 2 October, it made its first commercial flight for Aeroflot between Moscow and Tallinn in the Estonian SSR. While international services followed in April 1964, first to Warsaw and then to Helsinki, Stockholm and Vienna, the Tu-124 mainly flew domestic routes and was a modest success, with 163 produced, thirteen of which were exported.

It was the An-24, however, that became Aeroflot's regional workhorse. With between 44 and 50 seats and an excellent dirt-runway capability, the twin-turboprop plane was introduced on 31 October by Aeroflot's Ukraine Directorate, flying the route between Kiev and Kherson.

In 1970, a Soviet aircraft became involved in the first successful hijacking from the USSR to another country. Hijackings were becoming frequent events worldwide during this period, with more than 130 cases between 1968 and 1972 in the US alone. At noon on 15 October, an An-24B of Aeroflot's Georgian Directorate took off from Batumi en route to Sukhumi on the Black Sea coast, with 46 passengers and five crew members (two pilots, a flight engineer, a navigator and an air stewardess) on board. Among the passengers were Lithuanian national Pranas Brazinskas, who had been imprisoned twice previously for financial irregularities, and his teenage son. Five minutes into the flight, one of them handed a letter to the stewardess, Nadezhda Kurchenko, stating their intention to hijack the plane and defect to the West. They also produced a firearm and a grenade. While trying to prevent them from entering the flight deck, the stewardess was shot twice at point blank range and killed. The shooting continued, wounding the captain, navigator and flight engineer. Held at gunpoint, the injured crew reset course for Trabzon in Turkey, where the hijackers surrendered and were arrested. The following day, the passengers returned to the USSR on a military plane and a few days later the bullet-damaged An-24 was flown to Kiev for repair.

Eventually the aircraft was returned to service, its cabin decorated with a photograph of a smiling Nadezhda Kurchenko. After the collapse of the USSR, the repaired plane continued to fly for Uzbekistan Airways until it was finally retired in 1997. The Kurchenko Park in Sukhumi, with a monument to the stewardess, bears her name. The hijackers were tried and imprisoned in Turkey, and while

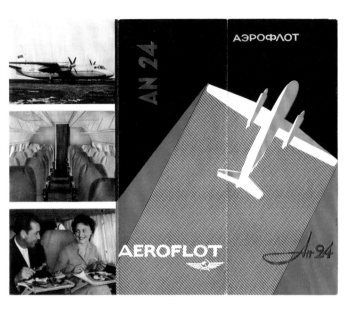

Promotional brochures for the Antonov An-24, early 1960s.

Promotional brochures for the Tupolev Tu-124, early 1960s.

Loading cargo on to a Tu-124 with a belt loader. The Soviet flag was a prominent feature of Aeroflot airliner livery after the introduction of the Tu-104, early 1960s.

the USSR sought to have them extradited to face criminal charges, the US sought to prevent it. After spending two years in prison, they were released and eventually gained the right to reside in the US, a move that was condemned internationally, particularly by the Soviet authorities, who criticised America for providing asylum to terrorists. Following this tragedy, the USSR took preventive measures: reinforced flight-deck doors were installed; ticket sales were restricted to passport-holders; and the selective screening of passengers' luggage was introduced. Between 1971 and 1980, plainclothes police officers flew in Aeroflot aircraft passing close to Soviet borders.

The Antonov An-24 aircraft became extremely popular, with a total of 1,367 units manufactured. By the time production stopped in 1979, both the Tu-124 and its big brother the Tu-104 were about to be taken out of service, but the reliable Antonovs were still flying 978 Aeroflot routes, transporting about 30 per cent of the airline's passengers. They continued in service for Aeroflot until the end of the Soviet era, afterwards being used by many of the post-Soviet airlines, with several still flying today. Over the years, several new variants were developed including the An-30 (adapted for aerial cartography), the An-26 (for cargo) and the An-32 (a more powerful transport version).

'Pcholka' [Little Bee] avion An-12. Aviaexport promotional brochure for the Antonov An-14, mid-1960s.

Another Antonov creation was the An-14 Pchelka (Little Bee). This was a small, six-seater STOL (Short Take-Off and Landing) utility aircraft first conceived in the mid-1950s. Although its maiden flight took place in 1958, full production did not start until 1965. Some 330 were built at the factory in Arsenyev in the Far Eastern USSR, most of which went to the Air Force. The An-14 proved too small for Aeroflot and only about 20 were used in the Moscow Directorate during a brief period between 1968 and 1970.

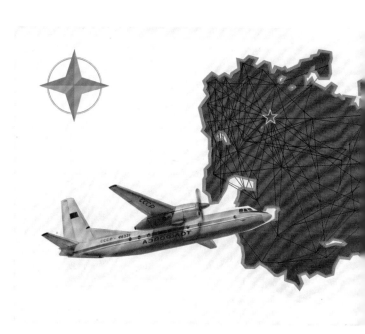

СХЕМА
РЕГУЛЯРНЫХ
МАРШРУТОВ,
ОБСЛУЖИВАЕМЫХ
САМОЛЕТАМИ АН-24

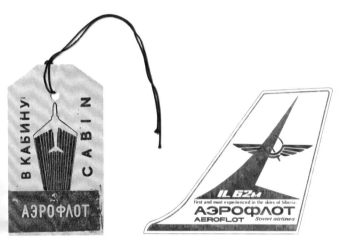

top: **Map of Regular Routes Served by the AN-24 Aircraft**. Brochure *Aircraft of the Antonov Design Bureau*, 1977.

left to right: Cabin luggage label, c.1970; ID tag, mid-1960s; VIP label used on the luggage of foreign guests arriving in the USSR at the invitation of the Central Committee of the CPSU, c.1975; cabin luggage label, 1960s; self-adhesive label Il-62M, c.1975.

A new long-range flagship jet: Il-62

The Tu-114 had been in service for less than two years when on 3 January 1963, the Il-62, a long-range airliner from the Ilyushin Design Bureau, made its maiden flight. Because the Tu-114 was near the beginning of its lifespan, the Ilyushin engineers had time to improve the Il-62 rather than rushing it prematurely into production. By summer 1965, a third prototype with new NK-8-4 engines had been completed and it was this version that went into mass production. As with any other new type of Soviet aircraft, thousands of cargo hours were flown before approval was given for passenger services.

The first regular flight, on 8 September 1967, left from Domodedovo (in Moscow) and landed in Alma-Ata (in the Kazakh SSR). A week later, the Il-62 replaced the Tu-114 on the international service between Moscow's Sheremetyevo airport and Montreal. The new flagship offered improved comfort, including remarkably low levels of cabin noise, for up to 186 passengers. However, fuel consumption was significantly higher than for its predecessor, with the Il-62 burning on average 17,960 lbs per hour. This meant it often failed to meet its required flight range, especially on long westbound routes with strong headwinds, and flights from Tokyo to Moscow were regularly forced to make an additional fuel stop at Novosibirsk, leading to

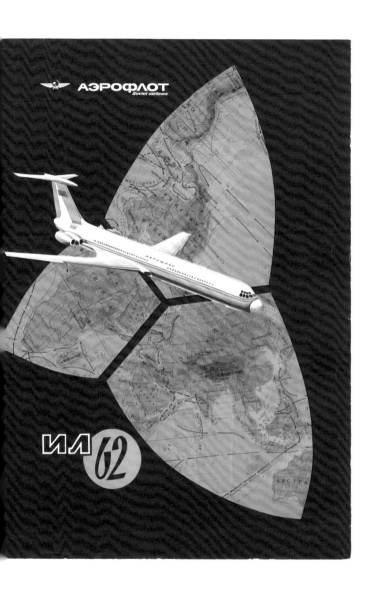

left: On board an Ilyushin Il-62. Promotional brochure, c.1970.

above: **Aeroflot IL-62**. Promotional brochure for the Ilyushin Il-62, c.1970.

above: An Il-62 at Moscow Sheremetyevo. Behind stands a JAL Japan Airlines DC-8, Aeroflot's competition on the Tokyo route. Aviareklama brochure, c.1970.

top right: **Only Aeroflot takes you directly from Rome to Moscow, without intermediate stops, with the biggest and most modern four-engine jet in just over three hours**. Italian brochure, 1967.

bottom right: **Aeroflot Il-62**. Promotional brochure, c.1970.

long delays and missed connections. This caused Aeroflot to lose passengers to its Japanese competition, which used the Douglas DC-8. The same problem occurred between Rabat (in Morocco) and Havana, a route that typically required an extra stop at Bermuda or Nassau.

To improve flight range, the Ilyushin Bureau made extensive modifications: aerodynamics were significantly improved; more economical and powerful Soloviev D-30KU engines were fitted; and fuel capacity was increased by almost 1,100 gallons. The Il-62M (M for modified), which burned some 1,540 lbs less fuel per hour, entered Aeroflot passenger service on 8 January 1974. A total of 193 aircraft were built and the model proved very reliable, continuing to fly for Aeroflot well beyond the Soviet era before finally being phased out in 2002. The Il-62M is still used by the Russian Air Force, North Korea's Air Koryo and Rada Airlines in Belarus.

AEROFLOT

LINEE AEREE SOVIETICHE

IL
62

SOLO L'AEROFLOT VI PORTA DIRETTAMENTE DA ROMA A MOSCA
SENZA SCALI INTERMEDI
COL PIU' GRANDE E COL PIU' MODERNO QUADRIREATTORE
in poco più di 3 ore

top: Yak-40 toy tin aeroplane, 1970s.

bottom: Children's tin lunchbox decorated with an illustration of an Il-18. The round ends show the Aeroflot logo while on the reverse side three Tu-104s are silhouetted. Norma factory, Tallinn, Estonian SSR, 1961.

top: Il-62 toy tin aeroplane, 1970s.

bottom: **Polet** (Flight). Game created by the Ilyushin Design Bureau for children aged 10-14 years. Moscow Toy Factory, 1987.

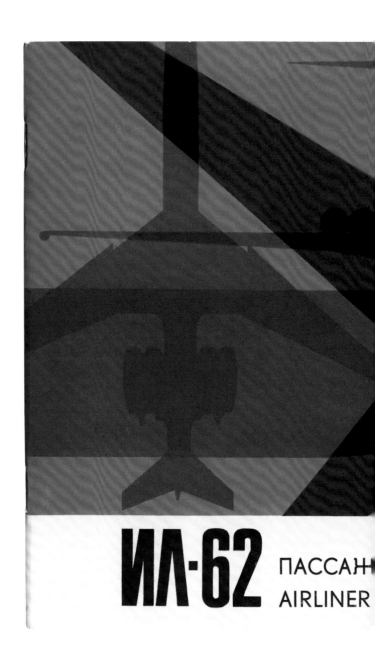

ИЛ-62 ПАССАН AIRLINER

IL-62 Passenger Plane. Bilingual Russian-English Il-62 sales brochure, produced for Aviaexport, c.1968.

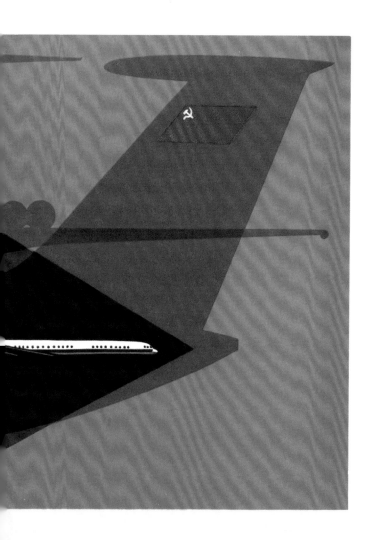

САМОЛЕТ

V/O · AVIAEXPORT ·

The next generation: Tu-134 and Yak-40

While on a state visit to France in 1960, Nikita Khrushchev had flown in the French Sud Aviation SE 210 Caravelle, the first jetliner with tail-mounted engines. This positioning meant the cabin was significantly quieter than that of the Tu-104, with its engines placed at the widest part of the wing near the passenger seats. On returning to Moscow, Khrushchev ordered Tupolev to develop an aircraft with a similar configuration. Using the Tu-124 as a starting point, Tupolev produced what would become the Tu-134, with the first prototype (at this point designated Tu-124A) making its inaugural flight on 29 July 1963.

An extensive test programme followed, with two more prototypes and several pre-production aircraft built, each successively modified and improved. Production began in 1966 and the first commercial passenger flight took place on 9 September 1967, travelling from Vnukovo (in Moscow) to Adler (in Sochi). Three days later, the Tu-134 made its international debut on the Stockholm route, quickly followed by services to other European capitals.

Between 1966 and 1984, a total of 852 Tu-134s were produced at factory 135 in Kharkov. Nicknamed 'Whistler' because of its high-pitched engine sound, the plane proved both popular and reliable. Accidents did occur, but it wasn't always technical issues with the aircraft that were to blame. On Saturday 11 August 1979, an air-traffic control error caused two Aeroflot Tu-134As to collide over Dneprodzerzhinsk (now Kamianske), an industrial city in the Ukrainian SSR. None of the 178 people on board the two planes survived, with casualties including members of the top Soviet football team, Uzbek Pakhtahor, who were flying from Donetsk to play against Dinamo Minsk. The other Tu-134A was en route from Voronezh to Chisinau, capital of the Moldavian SSR.

left: Aeroflot flight crew at Elista airport, North Caucasus. Postcard, 1979.

top: The two Tu-134 prototypes at Moscow Sheremetyevo airport. Aviaexport sales brochure, c.1966.

bottom: **Yak-40**. Aviaexport brochure for the Yakovlev Yak-40, c.1970.

Cover photograph from an Aviaexport brochure, 1965. At the Paris-Le Bourget Air Show the Soviets unveiled a whole range of new aircraft. Shown here: the Mi-6 CCCP-06174; the Mi-8 CCCP-06181; the Mi-10 (second prototype) CCCP-04102; the An-12B CCCP-11359; the Tu-124V CCCP-45072; the Il-62 (second prototype) CCCP-06176; the Tu-134 (second prototype) CCCP-45076. In the centre is the An-24B CCCP-46791. Also present in Paris was the An-22 prototype CCCP-46191 and an Il-18D CCCP-75581 (not in the photograph). Standing on its own at the top is a Finnair Sud Aviation SE 210 Caravelle.

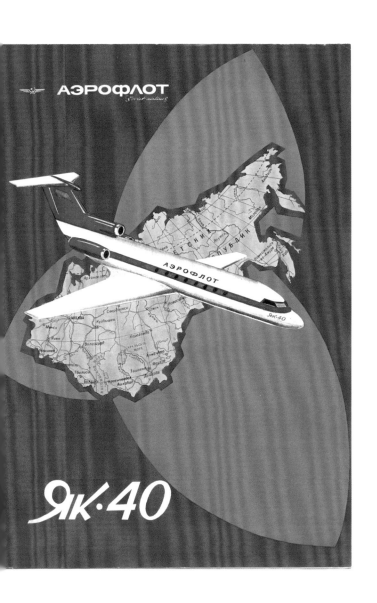

Aeroflot Yak-40. Promotional brochure, early 1970s.

By the time of the fall of the Soviet Union in 1991, these dependable aircraft had carried more than 550 million Aeroflot passengers. They remained in service in the post-Soviet era until the last Whistler was retired on New Year's Eve 2007, after more than 40 years of service, when flight SU754 from Kaliningrad touched down at Moscow's Sheremetyevo airport.

A small jet aircraft developed by the Yakovlev Bureau, capable of carrying between 24 and 32 passengers and with short and unpaved runway capability, the Yak-40 was a contemporary of the Tu-134. Introduced on 30 September 1968 on a flight of some 200 miles from Bykovo (in Moscow) to Kostroma, this regional jet was popular with both pilots and passengers. By 1975, Aeroflot already had 542 in service.

The Yak-40 was to become the first Soviet airliner to enter the Western European market. After its debut at the 1967 Paris Air Show, Aviaexport and the Yakovlev Bureau began a worldwide promotional campaign, flying the jet on demonstration tours in more than 80 countries in Europe and Latin America as well as to Japan, Afghanistan, Syria and the US. Of the 1,011 produced at factory 292 in the Volga port of Saratov, around 125 were exported including several to West Germany and Italy, making the Yak-40 the best-selling Soviet passenger jet of all time.

A giant freighter: Antonov An-22

In 1961, the Antonov Design Bureau began developing a strategic military aircraft capable of carrying bulky military vehicles and intercontinental ballistic missiles. The result was the An-22. Powered by the same engines as the Tu-95 and Tu-114, with a maximum take-off weight of 250 tons, it was at the time the world's largest aeroplane. Named Antaeus after the giant son of Poseidon and Gaia in Greek mythology, it became the star of the 1965 Paris Air Show.

Two prototypes were built at Svyatoshino airfield in Kiev, while general production took place in Tashkent, where 66 of these gigantic aircraft were manufactured. Despite often hauling heavy freight for industrial development and being painted in civil Aeroflot livery, all An-22 aircraft belonged to the Soviet Air Force and were flown exclusively by military crews.

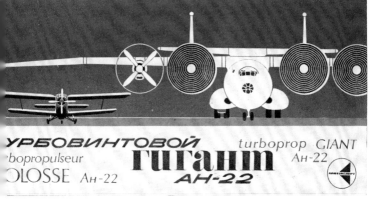

top: **An-22 Aeroflot**. Leaflet for the Antonov An-22, VDNKh (Exhibition of Achievements of National Economy in Moscow), 1969.

bottom: Multi-lingual (Russian, English, French) brochure for the 'Giant' An-22 published by Aviaexport, 1969.

The workhorse: Tu-154

Throughout the mid-1960s, Aeroflot operated three medium-range aircraft: the Tu-104, Il-18 and An-10. The supply of spare parts, trained crew and engineers for these three quite distinct planes proved a great strain on logistics. To increase operational efficiency and cope with increased passenger demand, it was therefore decided that all three should be replaced by a new type, the Tu-154.

This 164-seat jetliner was the first to be devised by the Tupolev Bureau specifically as a passenger aircraft, with no lingering connection to the design of strategic military bombers.

As with all Tupolev aircraft, the prototype was constructed in the on-site workshops adjacent to the Moscow design offices. After completion, it was disassembled and transported by road to the Zhukovsky airfield to begin its test programme.

The aircraft's maiden flight took place on 3 October 1968. Two years later, Aeroflot began using the Tu-154 to fly cargo, with passenger operations starting on 9 February 1972 (the airline's 49th birthday), flying between Vnukovo (in Moscow) and Mineralnye Vody, some 1,000 miles to the south. International services to Berlin's Schönefeld airport began on 2 April.

In 1974, following rigorous testing, the Chaplygin Siberian Scientific Research Institute of Aviation (SibNIA) in Novosibirsk discovered that the aircraft's wings were unlikely to last for even a quarter of its planned service life. Newly designed wings were fitted to no less than 96 aircraft, with the enormous cost of the operation, which would have bankrupted any commercial airline, being met by the Soviet state.

From the early 1980s, this enduring workhorse consistently accounted for half of Aeroflot's total passenger miles. It was exported to more than 20 countries and the exhaustively upgraded version, the Tu-154M, remained in production even after the break-up of the Soviet Union. Including all variations, a total of 923 units were built.

Unfortunately, the aircraft was also involved in the darkest day of Soviet aviation history. On Wednesday 10 July 1985, flight SU7425, a Tu-154B-2 from the airline's Uzbek Directorate, departed Karshi airport en route to Leningrad via Ufa. While cruising at 38,000 feet at too low an airspeed, it stalled, went into a flat spin, fell from the sky and crashed in the Uzbek desert, killing all nine crew members and 191 passengers. Investigators concluded that crew fatigue had been a major factor in the accident.

Aeroflot Tu-154. Promotional poster, 1970s.

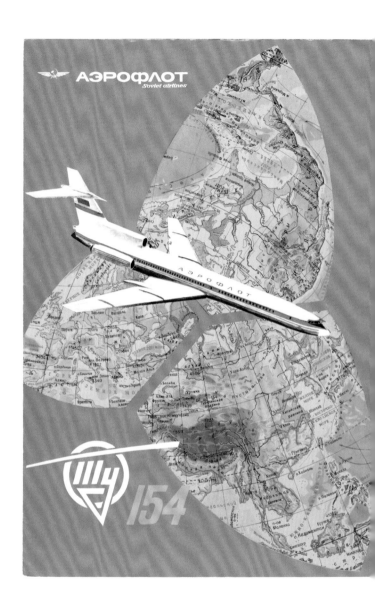

above: **Aeroflot Tu-154**. Promotional brochure published by Aviareklama, c.1972.

right: **Aeroflot Tu-154**. Self-adhesive luggage labels, c.1980.

Supersonic dreams: Tu-144

While Sputnik, the world's first artificial satellite, had won the space race for the Soviets in 1957 and Yuri Gagarin had become the first man in outer space in 1961, two other high-profile Cold War technological battles were still being fought: the race to put the first man on the moon and, somewhat closer to earth, the race to develop the first supersonic airliner. By the early 1960s, preliminary studies for supersonic transport undertaken in the late 1950s had developed into more concrete plans. In Europe, the British and French were collaborating to build Concorde, while in the US, a tender from several aircraft manufacturers was won by Boeing. In the Soviet Union, the colossal task was undertaken by the Tupolev Bureau.

The overly ambitious Boeing 2707 project quickly fell behind and by 1971 the Americans had abandoned their supersonic dream. But in the USSR, the entire Soviet aircraft industry soon became involved in the development of new materials, engines and construction techniques to overcome the enormous technological hurdles. Rivalry between the Concorde and Tupolev teams intensified as they became embroiled in Cold War espionage. In the late 1950s, the Soviets launched Operation Brunnhilde, a large industrial espionage offensive. Spies from Communist Bloc countries copied early French Concorde blueprints and technical documents on to microfilm. These were then smuggled out of the country on board the Ostend to Warsaw Express, hidden in toothpaste tubes and a sponge concealed behind a heating grill in the train's toilet. The films were subsequently picked up in Berlin by Stasi officers and sent on to Moscow.

French intelligence services uncovered the operation in 1964, when Sergei Pavlov, head of Aeroflot's Paris office, asked an airport worker to collect tyre scrapings from the Concorde test runway. After passing Pavlov a false rubber compound, the French placed him under surveillance. He was finally arrested on 1 February 1965, while meeting a contact in a restaurant in central Paris. His briefcase contained information on Concorde's landing gear, brakes and airframe composition. On the personal order of President de Gaulle, he was deported to the USSR, where he continued to work for Aeroflot, negotiating global air-traffic agreements. In his 2010 memoir Opening the World for Flights, Pavlov denies being a spy, claiming the alleged evidence was planted by French counterintelligence in a politically motivated operation intended to unsettle relations between France and the USSR.

Because the Concorde and Tupolev jets looked so outwardly similar, however, the Soviet aircraft was derisively nicknamed 'Concordski' in the West – though it might be fair to say that the general profile of such aircraft was largely dictated by the laws of

Aeroflot Tu-144. Promotional leaflet for the Tupolev Tu-144, VDNKh (Exhibition of Achievements of National Economy in Moscow), 1969.

Aeroflot Tu-144. Poster/leaflet depicting the prototype aircraft, 1970.

aerodynamics. In the event, the Tu-144 was larger and faster than Concorde and, underneath, proved to be a very different aircraft.

On 20 December 1968, the Soviet prototype was ready, but low clouds and dense fog prevented the first test flight. For ten long days the Tupolev team waited anxiously at Zhukovsky airport as the sky over Moscow remained grey with low visibility. Finally, on the last day of 1968, the sun broke through the clouds and Tupolev himself ordered the flight to proceed. The Tu-144 crew pushed the throttles forward and took off on a successful 38- minute flight. Tupolev had kept the promise he made to the Communist Party that the aircraft would fly in 1968, if only by a few hours. (The promise was reflected in the prototype's registration CCCP-68001, '68' indicating the year of the first flight.) This was a milestone, not just for aviation, but for the Soviet Union: it would be a full two months before Concorde would make its own maiden flight.

On 5 June 1969, the Tu-144 succeeded in breaking the sound barrier and a year later it became the world's first passenger airliner to exceed a speed of Mach 2.0. It was revealed to the West at the Paris–Le Bourget Air Show in May 1971.

Despite its initial success, the aircraft's high fuel consumption and consequent low range failed to meet Aeroflot's requirements and it was deemed unsuitable for use. The design was heavily modified to overcome some of the technical issues and after some 150 further

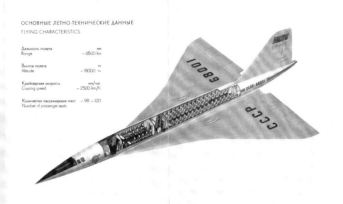

СКОРОСТЬ И КОМФОРТ · SPEED AND COMFORT

Poster/leaflet showing a cut-away view of the Tu-144 prototype's cabin, 1970.

test flights, the first production aircraft was presented at the Paris–Le Bourget Air Show in May 1973. However, on 3 June, during its second demonstration flight, the plane crashed, killing all six people on board and eight on the ground. While the exact cause of the crash remains undetermined, it was very likely the result of human error rather than faulty technology. Nevertheless, the accident was a huge blow for the Soviet supersonic programme and it was to be six months before test flights resumed.

By the mid-1970s, it had become apparent that the Tu-144 was not commercially practical and that its role would be little more than symbolic. On 26 December 1975, weekly route-testing flights were launched between Moscow and Alma-Ata in the Kazakh SSR, occasionally transporting mail and freight. A month later, on 21 January 1976, Concorde made its first passenger flight. To prevent its sonic boom from causing nuisance or damage on the ground, it was permitted to fly at supersonic speed only above the ocean – an impossible restriction for the Tu-144, which was flying overland from Moscow.

The launch of Soviet supersonic passenger operations coincided with the 60th anniversary of the October Revolution. The first flight departed from Moscow's Domodedovo airport on 1 November 1977, arriving in Alma-Ata two hours later, in half the time of a regular flight. The ticket price of 84 rubles (compared to 62 for the subsonic flight) covered only a fraction of the enormous operating costs but

a higher fare would have run counter to the Communist ideology of state ownership of property and production for the benefit of all. To cope with ever-increasing passenger traffic, Aeroflot required a large, economical aircraft, and by the time the Tu-144 had gone into service, the airline's advertising campaign was focusing on the imminent arrival of the Il-86 wide-body airliner.

By this time, alleged former spy Sergei Pavlov had been appointed Deputy Minister of Foreign Relations for Civil Aviation and was leading negotiations with Britain for regular flights for Concorde on the Trans-Siberian route to Asia. To reduce the impact of the sonic boom, the British argued that Concorde could fly subsonically over the European part of the USSR and supersonically over the sparsely populated regions east of the Ural mountains. In the event, permission to use Concorde over Soviet territory was not granted.

On 23 May 1978, a new version of the Tu-144 fitted with more efficient engines, designated Tu-144D, crash-landed during a test flight, killing two of its eight crew. The Tupolev Bureau immediately halted the trials and, in the absence of any pressing commercial need for such aircraft, supersonic passenger travel in the Soviet Union was over, having lasted for just seven months.

The two Tu-144 aircraft assigned to Aeroflot made only 102 flights for the airline, 55 of which had carried a total of 3,284 passengers. Although development continued, plans for new passenger flights were never realised. In 1983, with the economic crisis severely hindering Soviet aviation, the development programme was definitively cancelled, by which time a total of 20 Tu-144 aircraft had been constructed (four of which were used for static testing only).

left: Ded Moroz (the Russian Father Christmas) is pictured alongside a Christmas tree and a Tu-144. New Year greetings card, 1973.

above: The prototype Tu-144 being towed by an MAZ-541 truck (Minsk Avto Zavod, Minsk Car Factory) at Moscow Sheremetyevo, c.1969.

above: Aeroflot shoulder bag (265 x 190 x 125 mm) with a stylised image of the Tu-144, 1977.

top right: Cigarette pack bearing an image of the Tu-144, issued for Aeroflot's 50th anniversary. Java tobacco factory, 1973.

bottom right: Aeroflot Tu-144 souvenir ashtray (170 mm), early 1970s.

The Tu-144D continued to be used, mainly for scientific research and the delivery of urgent freight, between Moscow and Khabarovsk. The use of the aircraft as flying laboratories continued until 1990, with experiments including geophysical studies on the effects of focused sonic booms, ozone-layer investigations and training sessions for Buran spacecraft.

In the early 1990s, the American space agency NASA launched a study programme for the development of second-generation supersonic passenger aircraft and communication between the American and Russian aviation industries increased. For technical reasons, unhindered by political considerations, the Americans based their research on the Tu-144 rather than Concorde. They recognised that the Tu-144 more closely resembled the future of supersonic aircraft, being faster (Mach 2.35 vs Mach 2.2) and larger than Concorde, as well as cheaper to run. Significant flight data was gathered over 27 test flights between 1996 and 1998, but funding was still cancelled for the commercial supersonic airliner programme.

Of the seven Tu-144s still in existence, six are in Russia: one each at the Central Air Force Museum in Monino; the Ulyanovsk Museum of Civil Aviation; Kazan National Research Technical University; Samara University training airfield; and two at Zhukovsky air base. The seventh, in the Technik Museum Sinsheim in Germany, stands next to an Air France Concorde.

top and right: Tu-144 toy airplane and box. Produced at the Taganrog Mechanical Factory, named after Bulgarian leader Georgi Dimitrov, 1980.

above: Aeroflot Tu-144 postcard published for Air Fleet Day, late 1960s.

Beriev Be-30 versus LET L-410 and Antonov An-28

Less futuristic was the development of a replacement for the legendary An-2. The fourteen-seat Beriev Be-30 made its first flight on 8 July 1968 from the Beriev factory airfield in the port of Taganrog in the south-west of the USSR. Two other aircraft in the same class were simultaneously under development: in Czechoslovakia, manufacturer Let Kunovice was working on the LET L-410, while in the Ukrainian SSR, the Antonov Bureau was producing a successor to the An-14 Little Bee.

The L-410 took off on its maiden flight from Kunovice on 16 April 1969 and two weeks later, the An-14M, modified with turboprop engines, flew from Svyatoshino in Kiev. The small Antonov plane continued to evolve, resulting in the An-28, which took its first flight on 29 January 1973. By that time, the Beriev Be-30 programme had been cancelled in favour of the L-410, despite the former's excellent performance.

The purchase of the LET aircraft was a politically motivated act of support for the Czechoslovakian aviation industry, within the framework of the Council for Mutual Economic Assistance, an organisation established by the USSR in 1941 to further economic relationships between Communist nations. Aeroflot received its first deliveries in 1976.

It was not until October 1978 that the decision was made to commence mass production of the An-28 in Mielec, Poland. The aircraft didn't enter service until 1984, by which time several hundred L-410s were flying Aeroflot routes. Because of this late arrival, the An-28 saw limited use, being employed mostly in Siberia and in the hot and high-altitude conditions of the Tajik SSR.

Neither of these aircraft fully replaced the large numbers of An-2 planes, which continued to fly on many local routes and in their specialised roles in support of the national economy.

eft: Refuelling a LET L-410M of Aeroflot's Yakutia Directorate, early 1980s.

above: **Be-30 Aeroflot**. Promotional leaflet for the Beriev Be-30, only eight of which were ever manufactured. VDNKh (Exhibition of Achievements of National Economy in Moscow), 1969.

An An-28 of Aeroflot's Tajikistan Directorate, c.1986.

A new cargo aeroplane: Il-76

On 25 March 1971, a large new cargo aircraft, the Ilyushin Il-76, took off from the Khodynka airfield in Moscow, where the Ilyushin Design Bureau was based. Two months later, it was shown at the 29th Paris Air Show, where the Soviets had caused a sensation on so many previous occasions.

After its successful induction into the Air Force, an Il-76 made demonstration flights at Aeroflot's Tyumen Directorate in May 1975, transporting freight to the Samotlor and Nadym oil and gas fields of Western Siberia. Service with Aeroflot started in late 1976, and on 5 April 1977, the first commercial international cargo flight delivered 38 tons of vegetables to Sofia in Bulgaria. The Il-76 was soon making regular flights to Western Europe, replacing the An-12 on the route from Yokohama in Japan to Luxembourg, via Nakhodka, Vladivostok and Moscow. By the time of the Soviet Union's collapse, more than 80 of these versatile cargo transporters were in use by Aeroflot, with another 60 operated by other civil departments (such as the Ministry of Aviation Industry and several aircraft-design bureaus) and the majority in the service of the Soviet Air Force.

This successful model was exported to many countries, including China, India, Iraq, Syria, and Libya. With about 920 produced in Tashkent, and an upgraded version still in production in Ulyanovsk in Russia, the Il-76 is likely to remain in service for decades.

top: **IL-76 Aeroflot**. Luggage label depicting a Ilyushin Il-76, early 1980s.

bottom: Promotional leaflet published by Aviareklama, 1970.

above and right: **Aeroflot Yak-42**. Promotional brochures for the Yakovlev Yak-42, late 1980s.

A new passenger capacity: Yak-42

While the passenger capacity of the Tu-154 proved too large to make it economical for certain routes and airports, the Tu-134 was too small. A new airliner with room for 120 passengers was required to fill the gap. The Yakovlev Bureau embarked on the project in 1972, and on 6 March 1975, the first Yak-42 prototype took its maiden flight. Following a prolonged test and development period, the Yak-42 was brought into service with Aeroflot on 22 December 1980, flying from Moscow's Bykovo airport to Krasnodar in southern Russia. With lower fuel consumption than its predecessors, uncomplicated ground handling and a smaller flight crew (dispensing with the need for a navigator), the outlook for the aircraft was promising.

However, on 28 June 1982, a Yak-42 crashed en route from Leningrad to Kiev, killing all 132 people on board. When the investigation revealed the cause to be a structural defect in the stabiliser mechanism, all Yak-42s were grounded and production ceased. By the time the aircraft had been modified, production had restarted and flights had resumed on 12 October 1984, the economic and political climate of the Soviet Union had deteriorated. Production continued at a slow rate until the last model rolled off the Saratov assembly line in 2004. Throughout its lifespan, a total of 183 Yak-42 aircraft were built.

САМОЛЕТЫ
АЭРОФЛОТА

THE AEROFLOT
PLANES

САМОЛЕТЫ
АЭРОФЛОТА

THE AEROFLOT
PLANES

ПІЛЬГИ,
ПІЛЬГИ,
ПІЛЬГИ !

В осінньо-зимовий період на всіх повітряних лініях СРСР введено пільгові скидки з авіатарифу:

50% інвалідам, студентам, школярам, курсантам, аспірантам;

30% групам робітників, службовців, школярів та студентів (15 і більше чоловік), які вирушають в екскурсії.

Квитки оформляються за два дні до вильоту літака.
Інвалідам надається право позачергово придбати авіаквитки за десять днів до вильоту літака за розкладом.
Довідки можна одержати по телефонах: аеропорт Бориспіль — 25-22-52, аеропорт Жуляни — 72-12-01, Центральне агентство — 74-51-52.

Запрошуємо на повітряні траси!

ЦЕНТРАЛЬНЕ АГЕНТСТВО
ПОВІТРЯНИХ СПОЛУЧЕНЬ
УКРАЇНСЬКОГО УПРАВЛІННЯ
ЦИВІЛЬНОЇ АВІАЦІЇ

left: Postcard sets depicting the planes of the Aeroflot fleet, 1983.

above: **Benefits, Benefits, Benefits!** (in Ukrainian). Back cover of *Ukraine* magazine, December 1974.

above: **Aeroflot Il-86**. Brochure published by Aviareklama, 1986.

right: **SSSR Il-86**. The prototype aircraft is depicted flying over its birthplace, the Moscow Khodynka airfield, with the City Air Terminal complex in the foreground. Promotional brochure by the Ilyushin Design Bureau, c.1980.

Soviet wide-body airliner: Il-86

The popularity of air travel led to an ever increasing number of flights worldwide, causing congestion in both airspace and airports. To solve the problem, larger aircraft were being developed, requiring more powerful, high-bypass turbofan engines capable of delivering more thrust while burning less fuel. In January 1970, the famous American Boeing 747 became the first wide-body airliner to enter commercial service. This was followed by the McDonnell Douglas DC-10 in August 1971, the Lockheed Tristar in April 1972 and the European Airbus A300 in May 1974.

The Soviets also needed a wide-body aircraft to cover popular domestic routes from Moscow to Leningrad and Kiev, and to Black Sea resorts such as Simferopol, Sochi and Mineralnye Vody. The Ministry of Civil Aviation set the following specifications: the aircraft must be capable of carrying 350 passengers, have a minimum flight

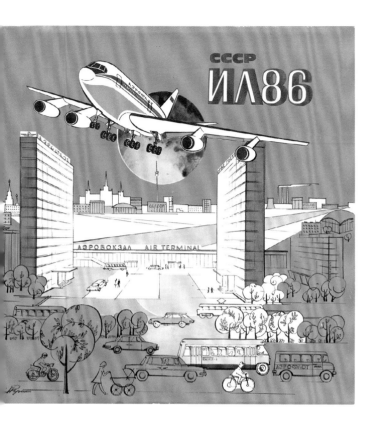

range of 2,250 miles, have a full payload of 40 tons, and be able to use 'B-class' airports with runways no more than 8,500 feet long.

Development of the Ilyushin Il-86 began in 1969. The designers intended to power the aircraft with four Soloviev D-30KU engines, but calculations showed that these could not deliver the required thrust: a fully loaded Il-86 would stall and crash if one of the outboard engines failed during take-off. The whole project began to fall significantly behind schedule, so the Ministry of Civil Aviation devised a back-up plan, arranging meetings between the Soviet and American aviation industries, where the Soviets proposed the foundation of a new American-Soviet aircraft-production plant for wide-body aircraft. While American aircraft manufacturers responded with varied interest, the scheme held little incentive for leading engine manufacturers General Electric and Pratt & Whitney since the US government had already sanctioned the sale of their high-bypass turbofan engines

(CF6 and JT9) to the USSR.

Both Boeing and Lockheed were keen to sell their B747 and L-1011 aircraft to the Soviets. In March 1974, Lockheed sent an L-1011 Tristar to Moscow for demonstration flights but while there was strong mutual interest, no agreement was reached. At this time, the USSR was experiencing great financial difficulties. As well as a number of Aeroflot's politically motivated routes proving unprofitable, a substantial increase in fuel prices outside the USSR meant hard-currency earnings had dwindled on international routes. In addition, the US government was unwilling to approve a joint plant for the construction of aircraft within the Soviet Union.

That same year, the Soviet Ministry of Aviation Industry ordered the Kuznetsov Design Bureau to develop an engine suitable for a Soviet-built wide-body aircraft. To save time and resources, the existing NK-8 low-bypass engine was upgraded to deliver the required thrust of 28,600 pound-force, with the new design renamed the NK-86. Further negotiations took place with both General Electric and Rolls Royce, with regard to supplying high-bypass engines for a possible long-range version of the Il-86, but these failed to yield results.

The first test flight of the Il-86 took place on 22 December 1976, and in June 1977 the plane was presented at the Paris Air Show. Aeroflot had hoped to fly the aircraft during the 1980 Summer Olympics in Moscow, but the test programme and technical flights had not yet been completed. The aircraft was eventually certified

left: **Il-86 Moscow – Berlin** (East Berlin). Luggage label, c.1982.

above: **Il-86**. Promotional brochure by the Ilyushin Design Bureau, c.1980.

on 24 December 1980 and departed two days later on its first passenger flight from Moscow to Tashkent. Despite the high fuel burn of its four NK-86 engines (6,600 lbs per hour each), it was relatively underpowered: within the Soviet aviation industry, the joke ran that the Il-86 was able to take off only because of the curvature of the earth's surface.

Nevertheless, the medium-range airliner was very reliable and ideal for Aeroflot's busiest routes. At the time, 49 of the USSR's 52 largest cities were less than 2,500 miles from Moscow and so within the aircraft's range. Many Soviet airports constructed in the late 1950s and early 1960s were struggling to cope with increased passenger numbers, so to reduce check-in times and the need for sophisticated ground-handling equipment, passengers entered the Il-86 via three airstairs built into the fuselage. This allowed them to drop off bulky luggage in the spacious lobbies below deck and proceed upstairs to the main cabin carrying only hand baggage.

The Il-86 flew to several European cities and by using fuel stops at Shannon airport in Ireland and Gander in Canada was able to fly long-distance to Havana and Lima. Routes to Buenos Aires were established, first via Budapest and Dakar, and later via Algiers, the Island of Sal (in Cape Verde) and Salvador (in Brazil). The plane also flew routes to Hanoi and Ho Chi Minh via Tashkent, Karachi and Kolkata. Production continued after the fall of the Soviet Union, ending in 1996, by which time 106 Il-86s had been manufactured.

Tu-204

"Tupolev" Joint-Stock Co.

Victims of time

A new generation of Soviet airliners, the Il-96, Tu-204 and Il-114 – successors to the Il-86, Tu-154 and An-24 respectively – were being developed in the 1980s and made their maiden flights before the end of the Soviet era. While these aircraft represented a huge technological step forward, they were adversely affected by the financial and organisational problems associated with the collapse of the USSR. Production remained slow and the limited numbers of aircraft manufactured meant they never became replacements for their predecessors.

Other victims of their time were the giant cargo aircraft of the Antonov Bureau – the An-124 and An-225. Developed from the An-124, the six-engine An-225 remains the heaviest aircraft ever built, with the broadest wingspan of any plane in operational service. It broke no less than 110 world records during an early flight on 22 March 1989 and made its public debut at the Paris Air Show a few months later. It had been designed to transport the Buran spaceplane and rocket boosters, but with the collapse of the Soviet Union this programme was cancelled and in 1994, the one and only An-225 was placed in storage and cannibalised for parts for the An-124.

Then in 1999, with the outsize air-cargo business booming, the An-225 was upgraded, returning to service in 2001. Still causing excitement wherever it lands, today it flies with Antonov's own airline, which specialises in cargo transportation. A second airframe, only partially completed, remains in storage in a hangar at Antonov's headquarters in Kiev.

left: Tu-204 sales brochure, early 1990s.

top: **Aeroflot Il-96-300**. Poster for the Ilyushin Il-96-300, c.1989.

bottom: **Antonov Design Bureau An-225 Dream**. Promotional brochure, c.1990.

Matchbox labels produced at Proletarian Banner matchbox factory, Chudovo, and
GIGANT matchbox factory, Kaluga, mid-1950s.
top: Aeroflot planes fly day and night; Riga – Moscow in 4 hours 30 minutes.
middle: Moscow – Leningrad 2 hours 35 minutes; Moscow – Tashkent 12 hours 40
minutes; Moscow – Kharkov 2 hours 40 minutes.
bottom: The aircraft is 5-6 times faster than the train; Moscow – Odessa 6 hours
35 minutes; Moscow – Yerevan 13 hours 15 minutes.

Matchbox labels, Gomel, Byelorussian SSR, 1962.

above: **Yak-24A Helicopter**. English, French, and Russian brochure for the 30-seat Yak-24A passenger version which never entered production, c.1960.

right: **Mi-1 Moskvich**. Brochure for the Mil Mi-1, published by Avtoexport, c.1961.

Helicopters

Along with its numerous aeroplanes, Aeroflot ran a large fleet of helicopters. Their main function was to assist the various national industries in building the economy, rather than passenger transport.

The first to be introduced was the Mil Mi-1, a light, three- to four-seater helicopter driven by a piston engine. Its inaugural flight took place in February 1954, when it was used by Aeroflot to deliver mail from the capital to several districts in the Moscow region. More than 2,600 were produced in Rostov-on-Don, Orenburg, Kazan and the State Aviation Works in Swidnik in Poland.

In September 1951, Stalin summoned leading aeroplane and helicopter designers to the Kremlin to instruct them to produce larger helicopters for both the Air Force and Aeroflot. The meeting resulted in a government decree that Mil should build a single-engine helicopter with a single rotor, capable of carrying twelve passengers, and Yakovlev a helicopter with a dual engine driving tandem rotors, with space for 24 passengers. Both aircraft were to be ready to fly within twelve months. The two bureaus raced to meet their deadline, with the Mil helicopter, later designated Mi-4, taking to the air on 3 June 1952, followed by the Yakovlev, designated Yak-24, a month later.

СССР-68131

Ми-1

Москвич

After lengthy state trials, the Yak-24 finally went into production in 1956. Susceptible to heavy vibration, it never achieved much popularity and its high maintenance requirements led to it being withdrawn from service in the first half of the 1960s, with only 40 having been built for the Air Force.

By contrast, the Mi-4, which entered service with the Air Force in summer 1953, was a great success. The standard version could transport sixteen people, while the passenger version, Mi-4P, was equipped with comfortable seats for up to eleven (later thirteen) passengers.

Aeroflot opened its first regular passenger helicopter route on the Crimean peninsula between Simferopol and the popular holiday resort of Yalta. Technical flights with Mi-4 helicopters started in November 1958 in preparation for the 1959 holiday season. Mi-4 helicopters were also used on the same route as flying construction cranes during the building of the world's longest trolleybus service, running 53 miles from Simferopol to Alushta and on to Yalta. In April 1959, Mi-4P helicopters began flying tourists to other Black Sea resorts of the Caucasus, travelling between Adler and Sochi, and later to Gagra, Khosta, Lazarevskaya and Gelendzhik. In their first season of full operation, the Black Sea helicopter lines carried some 45,000 passengers.

left: **Helicopter Kamov-18**. Presentation brochure, Brussels World's Fair, Soviet pavilion, 1958.

above: **Aeroflot**. Postcard with an illustration of a Mil Mi-4 flying above one of Moscow's Seven Sisters buildings, c.1960.

above: Mil Mi-4 promotional brochure showing two of its most active regions, Moscow and the Black Sea holiday resorts, Aeroflot, 1962.

right: A total of 3,409 Mi-4s were manufactured in Kazan until 1966. Promotional brochure published by Avtoexport, c.1959.

In total around one hundred Mi-4 routes were established across the USSR, mainly in Moscow, the Volgograd region, Siberia, Transcaucasia and the southern regions of the Azerbaijan and Tajik SSRs. The busiest route opened on 2 March 1960, between Baku in Azerbaijan and Neftyannye Kamni (also known as the Oil Rocks), the world's first offshore oil platform, 60 miles away in the Caspian Sea. Mi-4 helicopters loaded with passengers and perishables would make the 38-minute trip up to 25 times a day, carrying almost 400,000 passengers by 1965.

The Mi-4s were renowned for the wide range of tasks they performed. They flew thousands of sheep to new pastures in the Uzbek SSR, delivered food to starving reindeer in Kamchatka, transported building materials for the Patsknara River dam in Georgia and took live fish to fish farms near Vyshny Volochyok. They installed power lines on the Kola Peninsula and unloaded freighters at the polar harbour in Amderma. They were used in gas-pipeline construction across the USSR, geophysical surveys in the Krasnoyarsk and West Siberian Directorates, and made rescue flights in emergency situations. The Mi-4 remained in service until the early 1980s, when it was phased out and replaced with the larger, turbine-powered Mi-8.

HELICOPTER

ВЕРТОЛЕТ Ми·4

HÉLICOPTÈRE

В/О АВТОЭКСПОРТ · СССР МОСКВА

Вертолет

B·10

Helicopter

В/О·АВИАЭКСПОРТ·СССР·МОСКВА

CRUE - VOLANTE

МИ 10

Far rarer than the Mi-6 was the Mi-10 flying crane, of which 55 were built in Rostov-on-Don between 1964 and 1977 (17 of these were Mi-10K variants, with a shorter landing gear). A single Mi-10 was exported to Petroleum Helicopters, Inc. in the US. Shown here are various promotional leaflets from the early to mid-1960s. Clockwise from top left: V-10; Mi-10; Mi-10; V-10; Mi-10.

ÉLICOPTÈRE ◆ HELICOPTER ◆ ВЕРТОЛЕТ   МИ10

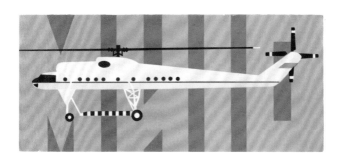

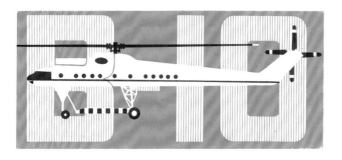

The smaller Kamov Ka-15, the world's first mass-produced co-axial helicopter, entered the Aeroflot fleet in 1958. Originally developed for the Soviet Navy, this two-seater aircraft (accommodating a pilot and one passenger) was used by Aeroflot mainly in agriculture, but was also stationed on icebreakers and fishing vessels to be used for scouting patrols. In 1959, the Ka-15 was joined by the Ka-18, capable of transporting three passengers and used mainly as an air taxi or ambulance. The Kamovs remained in use by the agricultural industries of the Moldovan and Kazakh SSRs until the mid-1970s, when they were replaced by the Ka-26.

Successful as they were, these light utility machines were just the beginning of Soviet helicopter development. The Mil Design Bureau became world-renowned in this field, achieving unprecedented technical advances. In 1957, only nine years after the arrival of the small-scale Mi-1, a truly gigantic helicopter, the Mi-6, was revealed. The first Soviet turbine-powered helicopter to go into production, this mammoth aircraft had a maximum take-off weight of 41 tons, could lift twelve tons, and could fly at speeds of more than 185 mph, smashing all previous helicopter performance records. In April 1966, it had the opportunity to demonstrate its outstanding capabilities in the Swiss Alps when it transported and positioned

top: **Helicopter Mi-6P**. Artist's impression of the giant Mil Mi-6P, capable of carrying up to 80 passengers. The only one ever built was demonstrated at the 1967 Paris Air Show. Avtoexport brochure, 1960s.

bottom: **Mi-6**. A total of 928 of these giants were built. Aviaexport brochure, 1960s.

some 40 concrete power masts, a large cable car and a steel truss in a matter of days – a project that would have taken several weeks by conventional means.

A variation of the Mi-6 was the Mi-10. Both these rotary-winged giants, known as the 'labourers of the sky', were primarily used by Aeroflot to assist in the development of the oil and gas industries in Siberia. Essentially flying cranes, they were also used for the installation of television and radio relay masts and pylons carrying high-voltage power lines.

The first-generation of piston-driven helicopters was gradually retired as larger turbine-powered versions were brought in. The eight-seater Mi-2 replaced the Mi-1 and the immensely popular, 28-seater Mi-8 replaced the Mi-4. The Soviets dominated the 1965 Paris Air Show, unveiling their Mi-8, Mi-6 and Mi-10 helicopters, alongside the Antonov An-22. The Mi-8 was widely exported and updated versions are still in production today.

Another interesting design was the Kamov Ka-26, which made its first flight in 1965 and its international debut at the 1967 Paris Air Show. This extremely versatile twin-piston helicopter could be fitted with interchangeable units: a six-seater passenger cabin (with space for an additional passenger in the cockpit), a cargo platform and a heavy-duty cargo hook for shifting loads or carrying crop-spraying equipment. Generally used in agriculture, it also performed numerous other operations including geological surveying, construction, search and rescue, ice and fish reconnaissance and motorway patrols.

left: **Mi-26**. Text on the sticker reads: **Science and Technological Progress 1985 / VDNKh SSSR**. With a payload of 20 tonnes, the Mi-26 remains the world's largest mass-produced helicopter. Brochure published for the VDNKh (Exhibition of Achievements of National Economy in Moscow), 1985.

above: **Happy New Year!** Photomontage by artist V. Sveshnikova. Postcard, 1958.

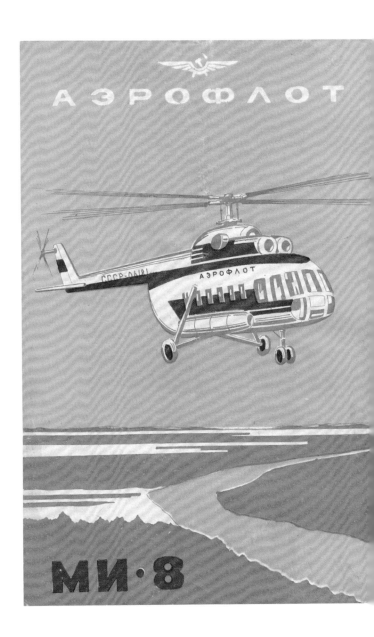

АЭРОФЛОТ

МИ·8

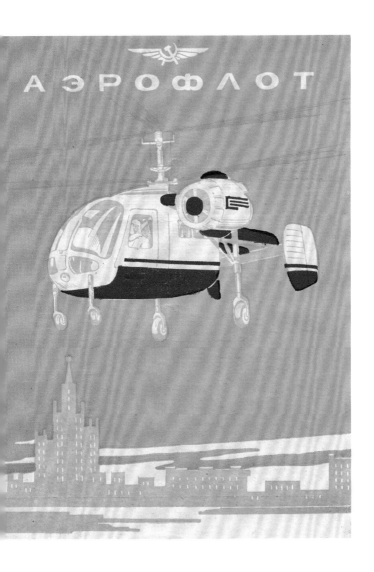

АЭРОФЛОТ

left: **Aeroflot Mi-8**. Still in production, and with more than 17,000 manufactured to date, the Mi-8 is the world's most popular helicopter. Leaflet for the VDNKh (Exhibition of Achievements of National Economy in Moscow), 1969.

above: **Aeroflot**. The versatile Kamov Ka-26, of which some 850 were built. Leaflet for the VDNKh, 1969.

В КОМАНДИРОВКУ, В ГОСТИ, НА ОТДЫХ– САМОЛЕТОМ БЫСТРО, УДОБНО, ИНТЕРЕСНО

8. FLY AEROFLOT!

The growth of the Soviet airline

The size of Aeroflot's domestic network grew from around 60,000 miles in 1945 to 225,000 in 1960 and 576,000 in 1985. During the 1980s, the airline regularly connected some 3,600 sites, from cities and small towns to villages and remote settlements, landing and taking off from central airports, regional airfields, dirt strips, agro-aviation fields, Arctic ice runways, river hydroports, and helipads.

Roads in the Soviet Union, largely made of dirt and cobblestones and often in poor condition, were no match for air travel, which gained in popularity from the late 1950s. Unlike in the US, car ownership was beyond the reach of most citizens so the proletariat travelled mainly via the extensive bus network. Buses, however, were often crowded and only the fortunate would find a seat. The slogan 'Fly Aeroflot Planes' must have appeared very attractive to travellers squeezed between other sweaty bodies in summer and frozen by the wind howling through the gaps in the doors in winter.

In 1950, journeys totalling 45.5 billion miles were made between Soviet cities: 91.1 per cent by rail, 5.4 per cent by water, 1.9 per cent by road and the remaining 1.6 per cent by air. By 1980, this figure had risen to 307.6 billion miles, of which 99.8 billion (32.5 per cent) were by air.

Flight schedules and fares were published in local newspapers twice a year. With airports conveniently located near city centres and villages, local routes regularly sold out, though undersubscribed flights were often peremptorily cancelled. Schedules were also subject to the weather, with heavy snowfall or dense fog causing delays, sometimes for days. Nevertheless, for several destinations, Aeroflot remained the only viable option.

This unpredictability, accepted as an inevitable part of Soviet air travel, was acknowledged in popular culture. The famous singer-songwriter, poet and actor Vladimir Vysotsky captured perfectly a sense of despair at one's circumstances and resignation that went along with Soviet air travel in his song 'Moscow – Odessa':

Yet again I'm flying Moscow – Odessa,
And again they won't let the plane take off.
But here comes the stewardess all in blue like a princess
As reliable as the whole civil air fleet.

Советские пассажирские самолеты

Soviet Passenger Aircraft. This set of ten postcards was published for Aeroflot's 40th anniversary in 1963.

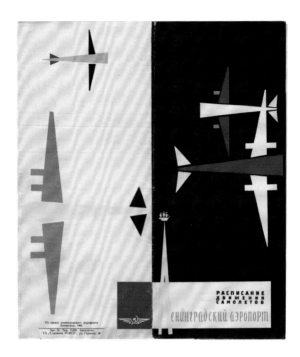

above: **Aircraft Timetable Leningrad Airport**. Leaflet, 1962.

right: **Aeroflot Tariffs and Times for Kiev Flights**. Leaflet published by the Ukraine Directorate, 1964.

I need to go to where there are blizzards and fog,
Where tomorrow they say it will snow!
They've opened London, Delhi, Magadan,
They've opened everything, but that's not where I need to go!

I was right – I could laugh, I could cry – the flight is delayed yet again
And they're taking us back to the past.
Slender as a 'Tu', that stewardess Miss Odessa,
Is just like the entire civil air fleet.

There's another delay until eight
And the citizens obediently doze...
I've had enough, to hell with it all,
I'll fly to wherever they'll take me!

(Verses 1, 10, 11, 12)

В КИЕВЕ
Все справки по телефону
Б 2-12-01
Б 2-12-02
Б 2-12-03
Можно заказать билет
с доставкой на дом
или на работу, тел. Б 9-55-78

Украинское территориальное
агентство воздушных сообщений

БФ 29258.   Зак. 306—5000, 25-2 64 г.
Киев, Крещатик, 44. Типография УУ ГВФ.

ТАРИФЫ
и ВРЕМЯ

More than 96 per cent of Aeroflot's traffic was within the USSR, not least because citizens required the permission of the Soviet authorities to travel abroad, with exit visas available only to prominent Communist Party members, diplomats, writers, artists and athletes or to those planning business trips prearranged by their employers. For the majority of citizens, the application process was so difficult that foreign travel was not considered a realistic option.

Domestic ticket prices set by the government had been reduced in 1956, when airfares were aligned with train fares, calculated in direct relation to the distance travelled. In addition, many passengers were entitled to concessions: a 10 per cent discount was commonplace for return flights; fares were reduced for students and groups; discounts of 50 per cent were given to children aged between five and twelve and those under five flew free of charge. These incentives, combined with the vast distances involved and the slowness of alternative means of transport, made air travel very popular.

above and right: **Aeroflot. On Holiday and to the Resorts by Plane**. Folder, 1960s.

A well-known Soviet phenomenon was the 'glass ticket', whereby passengers would bribe their way on to an aircraft with a 'gift' for the check-in officer or flight crew. Typically, this would take the form of money, a bottle of vodka (hence the name) or some similarly valuable item. If the check-in officer or crew knew the passenger well, sometimes no gift would be needed. Glass tickets were used mostly in rural settlements with small airfields, where everyone knew everyone else and would help each other out.

At larger regional airports and city airports, aviation workers and those with connections to airport employees could also use a glass ticket. A stranger, on the other hand, would need charm and charisma to convince the check-in officer (almost always female), with the chance of success at a large airport almost zero. In the end, everything depended on whether the check-in officer could make a deal with the captain, though many never allowed any violation of the rules.

АЭРОФЛОТ

In the busy summer holiday season, people would overcome the difficulty of obtaining tickets by making deals to pay double or triple the standard fare. As a result, planes often carried up to ten extra passengers, along with their luggage, adding anything up to a ton and a half of additional, unregistered weight. These passengers would be seated in the luggage compartment or on the flight attendants' folding seats, an arrangement easier to organise in planes with rear luggage compartments on the same floor as the passenger cabin, such as the Tu-134 or An-24, but more difficult in planes such as the Tu-154. Today, such practices would be unthinkable. In similar fashion, flight crews returning from Soviet Central Asian Republics would supplement the meagre official fruit supply by carrying considerable amounts of unregistered melons, tangerines, grapes and so on, to be distributed to family and friends or sold on the black market.

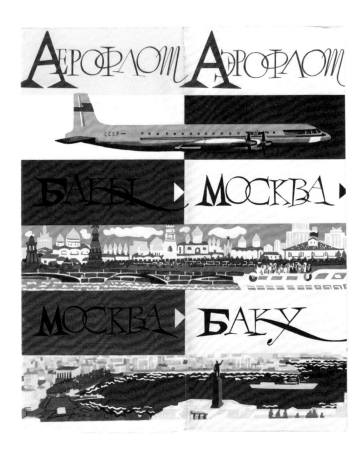

From its beginnings, Aeroflot operated only single-class aircraft on its domestic network and it can therefore be considered to be the world's first national low-cost airline. This situation changed in 1978, when a first-class service was introduced on a limited number of Tu-154 routes to Sochi, Mineralnye Vody and Simferopol, followed on 1 August by an all first-class service from Moscow to Khabarovsk in the far east, using Il-62s with 144 seats (instead of the usual 168 to 186), with fares 20 per cent higher than standard.

Regular domestic inflight service was poor in comparison with that offered on international routes. Passengers joked that the only explanation for the scrawny, rubbery chicken served as part of the inflight meal – nicknamed 'Aeroflot hen' – was that the stuff was mass produced in a secret state factory.

left: **Aeroflot. Baku-Moscow/Moscow-Baku**. Brochure from 1959 announcing the introduction of a new Il-18 service between the two cities starting on 20 June. The Ilyushin took 3 hours 40 minutes, fifteen times faster than the express train.

top: **Aeroflot Azerbaijan Directorate**. Brochure, 1961.

bottom: **Aeroflot SSSR** [arriving at] **Sverdlovsk** [departing from] **Moscow Central airport**. Luggage tag, 1950s.

Dorozhnyy [Road] **chocolate**. Produced by Karl Marx confectionery factory, Kiev, early 1970s.

Publicity and promotion

In the absence of competition, and with aviation part of the public transport network, the state did not need to spend much money on advertising. For instance, between 1957 and 1959, when passenger numbers increased by about 7.5 million, Aeroflot produced only 5 million items of printed promotional material, of which a million copies were published by the local directorates. Revenue targets were set out in the five-year plans, with funds distributed among Aeroflot's subdivisions according to four key factors: the volume of traffic in the previous year; the number of passengers relative to the local population; the growing demand for air-transport services in the region; and the quantitative and qualitative composition of the fleet.

While Aeroflot attempted to follow the Marxist precept of supplying a product sufficient to the needs of the population, the introduction of larger An-10 and Il-18 airliners in 1959 led to excess capacity. Surveys of Moscow's citizens showed many were still using long-distance trains and were only vaguely aware of the advantages of air travel in terms of time saved, low fares and free baggage allowances. Cheaper airfares were introduced and the quantity and range of advertising material expanded to include colourful brochures, posters, postcards and magazine slots. Each directorate was responsible for fulfilling its assigned traffic targets, and between 1960 to 1962, the overall amount of promotional literature increased to 33 million copies. In 1962, Aeroflot spent 1 per cent of its income on advertising, in comparison with Pan Am's 6 per cent and Air France's 7 per cent.

top: Aeroflot plastic cups decorated with paper wraparounds, 1970s.

bottom: Members of the Aeroflot advertising office in Rostov-on-Don discuss a new campaign, from the book *A Day with Aeroflot*, 1973.

Sergey Georgievich Sakharov, who worked in advertising from the mid-1930s to the early 1960s and was recognised as an Honoured Artist of the Russian Soviet Federative Socialist Republic in 1957, was perhaps best known for penguin and seal characters used to promote Soviet ice-cream, as well for posters for vodka, cigarettes and fruit juice. However, he also designed several posters and brochures for Aeroflot, including 'Air Routes to the Resorts of the Caucasus', 'Air Routes to the Resorts of Crimea', 'Moscow – Tashkent', 'Moscow – Tbilisi', 'Moscow – Alma-Ata' and 'International Air Routes of the Soviet Union'.

Soviet advertising – including that for Aeroflot – often created an illusion of abundance and choice that did not really exist. The famous slogan 'Fly Aeroflot Planes' was intended not to promote Aeroflot as a company better than its rivals – after all, there were no other airline options for Soviet citizens – but to persuade people of the usefulness of flights, particularly in the post-war period when rail travel was the main competition. Accordingly, slogans focused on the benefits of flying: 'Short travel time – long vacations' or 'Remember! You will reach the resorts of the Crimea and Caucasus on the same day you leave Moscow'. Over time, domestic advertising became less a matter of enticing customers than of communicating factual information about the advantages of air travel.

АЭРОФЛОТ

СОЧИ · SOCHI

far left: **To the Holiday Resorts of the USSR by Aeroflot**. Luggage label, 1969.

left: **Aeroflot**. Postcard published by Vneshtorgizdat, Odessa, 1969.

above: **Aeroflot. Sochi**. Brochure, early 1960s.

top: **Aeroflot**. Information folder, early 1960s. A Tu-104 is silhouetted in the centre panel; the left panel shows landmarks of Moscow and Kiev; the right panel depicts Kiev's Zhulyany airport building, with passengers boarding an An-10, beneath which an Il-18 is being loaded with cargo.

bottom: **Aeroflot. On Business Trips by Plane**. Information folder, early 1960s.

top: **Aeorflot. Aircraft Timetable for Flights to the Holiday Resorts**. Leaflet, c.1960.

bottom: **Aeroflot. Cargo Transport by Plane**. Leaflet, early 1960s.

above: **Aeroflot. Western Siberia**. Leaflet promoting flights in one of Aeroflot's 29 territorial directorates, c.1964.

top right: **Cherish your rest time! On holiday and to the resorts – by plane!** Fold-out brochure with the Baltic and Black Sea resorts marked on the map, early 1960s.

bottom right: Map of Moscow with its four airports: North: Sheremetyevo, West: Vnukovo, South: Domodedovo, East: Bykovo. The City Air Terminal is shown in the centre. Aeroflot promotional brochure, 1964.

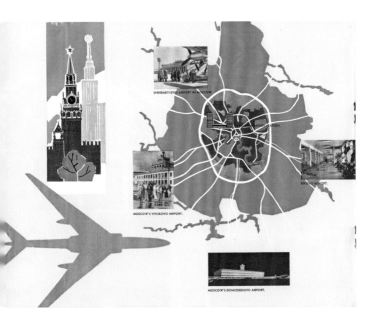

MOSCOW'S VNUKOVO AIRPORT.

MOSCOW'S DOMODEDOVO AIRPORT.

Moscow and its airports

With its several airports – and as the nation's capital – Moscow was the air transport centre of the Soviet Union. Its first airport, named after Bolshevik leader M. V. Frunze, was officially opened on 3 October 1910, with regular passenger flights launched when the Deruluft route to Königsberg opened in 1922. It acquired its colloquial name Khodynka from its location at the Khodynka field, just four miles from the Kremlin. Several leading aircraft design bureaus including Sukhoi, Mikoyan, Ilyushin and Yakovlev established their headquarters and factories in the vicinity of Frunze.

Moscow's second airport, Bykovo, located to the south-east of the city, opened in 1933, with regular flights starting in 1936, when Frunze was temporarily closed for reconstruction. A third airfield, Vnukovo, was built in the south-west of the city and at the outbreak of war in 1941, it was put to military as well as civil use. Shortly after the war, the aviation authority decided to transfer all flights from Frunze to Bykovo and Vnukovo, with the latter becoming the USSR's new principal civil airport.

left: **Aeroflot. Main office for Air Transport Services** with a photograph of Moscow's City Air Terminal, late 1970s.

top: Moscow City Air Terminal leaflet, early 1960s.

bottom: Luggage label, 1960s.

Памятка

ПАССАЖИРА,

ВЫЛЕТАЮЩЕГО ИЗ АЭРОПОРТА ВНУКОВО

left: Aeroflot. Passenger Information for departures from Vnukovo airport, 1956.

above: **Aeroflot will take you to any corner of the country.** Depicting the An-24 prototype SSSR-L1959 in its first livery. The landmarks at the bottom are the Hotel Ukraine in Moscow (left) and Hotel Moscow in Kiev (right). Advertisement published by the Ukraine Directorate in *Construction and Architecture* magazine, December 1962 (one month after An-24 flights began).

top left: **Aeroflot. Kyrgyzstan**. Brochure presenting Kyrgyzstan and its air routes, early 1960s.

bottom left: **Aeroflot. The Urals**. Brochure presenting the Ural region and its air routes, 1964.

above: *Ogonёk* magazine cover, 25 June 1961. Interior caption reads: **Flight attendant Tamara Beysenova has flown the routes of Kazakhstan for over a year. And finally, she has her first flight to Moscow on the Il-18 airliner.**

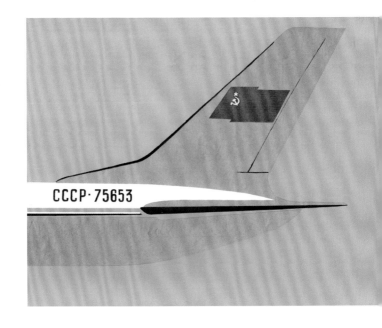

In the 1950s, with demand for air travel increasing, more capacity was needed. In July 1959, Soviet leader Khrushchev returned from a visit to London, landing at the new Central Aerodrome of the Air Force, formerly named Sheremetyevsky, to the north-west of Moscow. He praised London Airport (as Heathrow was then known) and its services, proposing that something similar be constructed for Moscow. Renamed Sheremetyevo, the military airport was handed over to the civil ministry, opening on 11 August with the arrival of a flight from Leningrad. Domodedovo, south-east of the city, was opened in 1962, with regular passenger services from 1964. Moscow now had four main civil airports, each named after its nearest village: Sheremetyevo for international and domestic flights heading north to Belarus and the Baltic states; Vnukovo for southbound flights to Ukraine, Moldova and the Transcaucasian republics; Bykovo for European regions of the country; and Domodedovo for destinations in Central Asia, Siberia and the far east.

In summer 1960, a helicopter station was opened at the old Khodynka airfield. From here, Mil Mi-4Ps and later Mi-8s operated regular passenger shuttle flights to Vnukovo, Sheremetyevo and Domodedovo. The Moscow City Air Terminal complex, incorporating

left: Tu-104 tail, Aeroflot booklet, 1964.

above: Three Yak-40s at Moscow Bykovo airport, Aeroflot Central Regions Directorate. From an Aviareklama brochure, c.1970.

above left: **Moscow. Aeroflot Hotel**. The hotel formed part of the Moscow City Air Terminal complex. Luggage label, c.1964.

above right: **Aeroflot**. Ukrainian-language label, 1964.

top right: Moscow Domodedovo airport. Aeroflot calendar photograph, 1967.

bottom right: Illustration from an Aeroflot Tu-114 brochure, c.1960.

the helicopter station, opened at Khodynka on 25 May 1965. Air passengers could check in, drop off their luggage and take a bus, taxi or helicopter directly to the aeroplane at their departure airport. (Ultimately proving uneconomical, the helicopter shuttle flights were curtailed in 1971.) The terminal processed up to 3,000 passengers an hour, substantially alleviating pressure on the four airports. In the foyer, passengers could familiarise themselves with their seat locations using large models of aeroplanes and helicopters and in the event of a long delay, transit passengers could watch a movie at the on-site cinema or even go into central Moscow. Following a huge drop in passenger numbers after the collapse of the USSR, the terminal eventually closed in 2004. While the central airport and air terminal no longer exist, the nearby metro station retains the name 'Aeroport'.

top: The Tu-154B CCCP-85192 at its home airport, Yerevan Zvarnots, 1985.

bottom: Postcard of Il-18 and An-24 at Ashgabat airport, Turkmen SSR, 1974.

top right: **Aeroflot. International Airport Borispol**. Brochure presenting the new international Kiev-Borispol airport, 1966.

bottom right: Passengers boarding a Yak-40 at Ulyanovsk.

международный
аэропорт
борисполь

АЭРОФЛОТ *Soviet airlines*

Irregular flights in the Arctic regions began in the 1920s and were organised in 1933 under the Main Directorate of the Northern Sea Route (Glavsevmorput). Arctic expeditions and sea-route patrol flights were very important for shipping in the Arctic and Soviet Far East. Glavsevmorput flight units were transferred from the Ministry of the Navy to the Main Directorate of the Civil Air Fleet (Aeroflot) in 1960, becoming the Polar Aviation Directorate in 1964, responsible for all flying activities in the territory. To improve services, Polar Aviation was disbanded in 1970 and its activities divided over several territorial directorates.

above: Photograph showing an Il-14 of the Polar Aviation Directorate, c.1965. The words on the plane read **Polar Aviation**.

top right: **Aeroflot. Polar Aviation**. Leaflet, c.1962.

bottom right: Back cover of an Antonov An-12 Aviaexport promotional leaflet published after the Antarctica flight expedition by an Il-18 and an An-12 during the winter of 1961-62.

Г 90315. Рекламбюро Аэрофлота. Изд. № 299. Типография им. К. Пожелы, г. Каунас, ул. Пушкина, 11. Зак. № 25.

АЭРОФЛОТ

ПОЛЯРНАЯ АВИАЦИЯ

МОСКВА
ПЕКИН

АЭРОФЛОП

Moscow-Peking. Aeroflot. Brochure cover, 1956.

International connections

Despite never encompassing more than 3.3 per cent of its passenger traffic, Aeroflot's international network was of great political importance. At the beginning of 1940, the airline operated routes to ten foreign countries: Königsberg, Danzig and Berlin in Germany; Stockholm in Sweden; Burgas and Sofia in Bulgaria; Riga in Latvia; Kabul in Afghanistan; and Ulaanbaatar and Altai Bulak in Mongolia.

With the German invasion in 1941, flights to Europe abruptly ceased, before being restored soon after the end of the war. In November 1946, the Moscow Air Group for International Services was established, running flights to thirteen international destinations: Belgrade in Yugoslavia; Berlin in East Germany; Budapest in Hungary; Bucharest in Romania; Warsaw in Poland; Vienna in Austria; Prague in Czechoslovakia; Sofia in Bulgaria; Tehran in Iran; Tirana in Albania; Ulaanbaatar in Mongolia; Helsinki in Finland; and Kabul in Afghanistan. However, growing political unrest restricted Aeroflot's international ambitions. For non-Soviets, travelling to the USSR was never more difficult than in the period between the end of the war in 1946 and Stalin's death in 1953, when anyone entering the country was viewed as a potential Western spy. Aeroflot's international flights and passenger numbers decreased, while foreign airlines were forbidden from entering Soviet airspace. Meanwhile, Aeroflot set up airlines in politically aligned countries, including China, North Korea, Mongolia, Poland, Hungary, Romania, Bulgaria and Yugoslavia.

top: International flights timetable, summer 1967.

bottom: *Civil Aviation* magazine cover, issue 8, August 1964.

Unused luggage tags to Rabat and Pyongyang, c.1972.

In 1955, the landscape of Soviet aviation changed. With Stalin dead and the Cold War beginning to thaw, air-traffic agreements were made between the USSR and other nations. Aeroflot's monopoly on flights between the USSR and Eastern European countries came to an end when LOT Polish Airlines began operating between Warsaw, Vilnius (in the Lithuanian SSR) and Moscow. This was followed by CSA Czechoslovak Airlines on the Prague to Minsk (Belarussian SSR) to Moscow route. In February 1956, Aero (renamed Finnair in 1968) became the first Western airline to fly to Moscow.

The introduction of the faster Tu-104 aircraft revolutionised long-distance Aeroflot services, epitomised by the journey between Moscow and Peking. Prior to the Tu-104's arrival the route was operated by the Ilyushin Il-14. Designated Aeroflot flight 135, the service operated six days a week, with a one-way ticket priced at 1,662 rubles plus 17 rubles for every kilogram of luggage. There were seven intermediate refuelling stops – in Kazan, Sverdlovsk, Omsk, Novosibirsk, Krasnoyarsk and Irkutsk, where the plane rested overnight before continuing the following morning to Ulaanbaatar and then to Peking, the final destination in a gruelling journey lasting 32 hours 10 minutes (as long as there were no delays).

Aeroflot. Moscow–Peking by Tu-104. Poster in Russian, Chinese and English. The illustrated landmarks are the Vodovzvodnaya Tower (Moscow) and the Forbidden City (Peking), 1959.

above: Flight attendants from the International Directorate with a Tu-114 model at Moscow Sheremetyevo airport. Aeroflot brochure, c.1964.

right: Passengers board a Tu-154B-1 at Novosibirsk, 1983.

In December 1956, the Tu-104 was introduced to the route. Designated Aeroflot flight 11, the service now departed every Wednesday and Sunday at 23:45, making only two refuelling stops, at Omsk and Irkutsk, before arriving at Peking at 15:30 local time (10:30 Moscow time), reducing the journey time to just 10 hours 45 minutes, three times faster than before. There was no increase in ticket price. This huge and sudden improvement should have been reflected in the new brochure for the service produced in 1957, but while the new plane and revised timetable were shown, the illustration of the seven intermediate landings of the Il-14 remained.

The introduction of the Tu-104 also enabled the Soviet Union to establish mutual landing agreements with Western countries. Direct Tu-104 flights to Brussels, Amsterdam and Paris opened in summer 1958, followed by London in May 1959. The respective national carriers, SABENA, KLM, Air France and BEA, flew a reciprocal service to Moscow.

International air fares, settled biannually at the International Air Traffic Association tariff conferences, were identical for airlines flying the same routes. In the late 1950s, Aeroflot had introduced two cabin classes on international services, with first-class fares 25 to 30 per cent higher than standard tourist class. Domestic air-transport deregulation began in the US in the late 1970s and within the EU in 1992, making competitive, market-based air fares a relatively new, post-Soviet phenomenon, particularly where international air traffic is concerned.

above: **Aeroflot. What you need to know. Mandatory rules for air passengers.**
Leaflet setting out instructions for passengers, 1978.

right: **Aeroflot. For passengers on international airlines** (in French). Leaflet with
information for passengers flying to the USSR on Aeroflot or using the airline's
flights to the Middle East and East Asia with transit in the Soviet Union, c.1970s.

POUR LE PASSAGER
DES LIGNES AERIENNES
INTERNATIONALES

left: **Moscow. Aeroflot**. Poster by artist Nikolay Litvinov, early 1960s.

above: **Krugozor** (Horizon). Cover of a monthly magazine containing six flexi-disks sewn between the pages. Illustration 'In the world of professions, Aeroflot' by S. Alimov, August 1974.

The 1960s saw a remarkable growth in Aeroflot's international network, most noticeably in establishing links with countries with a political connection to the USSR. Routes flown increased from only 9,400 miles in 1960 to 110,200 miles in 1970. New African destinations like Rabat (in Morocco), Accra (in Ghana), Conakry (in Guinea) and Khartoum (in Sudan) opened in 1962, as well as the first south-east Asian destination of Jakarta in Indonesia.

The most direct route for Western airlines wanting to fly to southeast Asia and Japan crossed Soviet territory, but permission to enter Soviet airspace was denied by the government, meaning airlines initially had to fly a much longer route via the Middle East and India. Later, as aircraft range improved, the polar route over the Arctic, with a fuel stop in Anchorage in Alaska, was introduced.

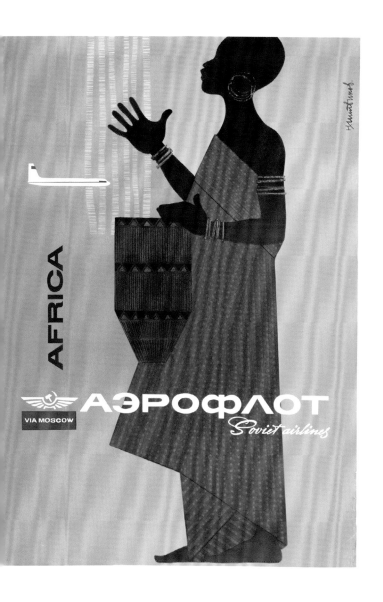

left: Advertisement announcing the new weekly service Moscow – Algiers – Conakry – Dakar by Il-62. *Soviet Union* illustrated monthly magazine, February 1969.

above: Poster promoting flights to Africa. Illustration by Nikolay Litvinov, early 1960s.

 THE FAR EAST

In 1966, after years of negotiation with Japan, Aeroflot's first joint international operation was launched. On 10 August, an Aeroflot Tu-114 made a technical test flight between Moscow and Tokyo; on 17 April 1967, the first regular passenger flight with mixed Aeroflot and Japan Airlines cabin crew took place. The Moscow to Tokyo leg, typically with a tailwind, took 10 hours 35 minutes, while the return flight with a headwind took 11 hours 25 minutes. To enhance comfort, two Tu-114 aircraft, both bearing Aeroflot and Japan Airlines insignia on their fuselage, had their cabins modified into a three-tier class system accommodating 116 passengers: 72 in economy, 32 in first class and twelve berths across four private compartments (known as coupés).

This joint operation lasted until 1969, after which the Soviets granted rights to Japan Airlines to fly DC-8s on the trans-Siberian route to Europe via Moscow followed by similar concessions for European carriers including Air France, BOAC, SAS, KLM and Lufthansa. Thanks to Moscow's geographic position and way the trans-Siberian route reduced flight time between Europe and Japan by approximately four hours, allowing substantial savings in fuel, Aeroflot was in a strong position to negotiate Fifth Freedom rights, whereby an airline may operate between foreign countries as part of a service connecting to its own country. In addition, charges for foreign carriers to fly over Soviet territory became a major revenue source.

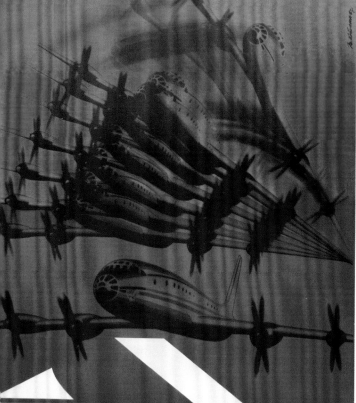

left: Aeroflot brochure presenting the Soviet Far East and its air routes, early 1960s.

above: Layered images of a Tu-114 form a 'Japanese fan' to promote the Moscow–Tokyo route. Poster, c.1967.

While the majority of Aeroflot's international flights originated at Moscow's Sheremetyevo airport, flights to Europe from other cities such as Leningrad, Kiev and Minsk grew steadily. On 15 July 1968, less than six years after the Cuban missile crisis, an Il-62 flew the first regular route between the USSR and the US, travelling from Moscow to Montreal and on to New York. Pan Am Boeing 707 aircraft flew the return service, with a stop in Copenhagen.

Another development was an agreement between Aeroflot and KLM Dutch Airlines that lasted from 6 April 1971 to 31 October 1972. During this period, Aeroflot Il-62 planes made 82 return flights from Amsterdam via Sheremetyevo to Tokyo, returning via the trans-Siberian route. Every Tuesday, an Il-62 with an Aeroflot cockpit crew and purser, alongside a KLM purser and three cabin attendants, departed from Amsterdam's Schiphol airport, while two weekly KLM flights to Tokyo used DC-8 aircraft following the polar route via Anchorage. The number of Aeroflot's international destinations increased year on year, so by summer 1973, the airline served 75 cities outside the USSR and by 1980, the network of international routes had grown to a total of 134,000 miles.

In 1975, Aeroflot began to use Ireland's Shannon airport – the westernmost non-NATO airport on the European side of the Atlantic – as a refuelling stop for its transatlantic flights. However, the oil crisis of 1977 led to soaring prices and Aeroflot, which had to pay for Western fuel with hard currency, was hit hard. As a result, Shannon lost some 200 flights a year of Aeroflot traffic. To counter this, Aeroflot

left: The mixed Soviet and Dutch flight crew of the first joint Aeroflot-KLM flight to Tokyo by Il-62. Amsterdam Schiphol airport, 1971.

above: **Time – the Deciding Factor!** The An-10 plane depicted here played a major role in Aeroflot's domestic network in the early 1970s. This changed abruptly following a fatal accident in 1972 (see pages 91–92). Back cover of *Ukraine* magazine, March 1970.

planes would take on as much fuel as possible in Moscow and fly directly to Gander in Canada, where fuel was 10 per cent cheaper and much less was required for the Il-62Ms to reach their destination in Havana. For Shannon, it was a financial nightmare, so Aer Rianta – the Irish state airport authority – devised a plan to convince Aeroflot to reverse its decision. In 1980, they built an airport fuel depot supplied with Soviet fuel delivered through the River Shannon estuary by tanker. For Aeroflot, home-produced fuel meant not having to spend hard currency; for Shannon, the arrangement brought increased landing charges, ancillary revenues and significant benefits for local businesses including handling agents, the fuel company and local hotels used for Aeroflot crew stopovers. However, progress stalled following the Soviet invasion of Afghanistan, with US President Ronald Reagan suspending all Aeroflot flights to the US from 5 January 1982.

left: Tu-114 luggage label, early 1960s. Following the introduction of the Il-62, the Tu-114 quickly disappeared from international service.

above: A sign of Soviet presence in Kabul, Afghanistan, 1980: Misha, Soviet mascot for the Moscow 1980 Olympics, and an Il-86 on a billboard advertising Aeroflot's weekly (and from August until October, twice weekly) service Moscow – Tashkent – Kabul. Aeroflot flight 531 was operated by Tu-154s while Ariana Afghan Airlines flew a reciprocal weekly service using Boeing 727s.

above: **Aeroflot invites you to Moscow – the capital of the 1980 Olympics!** Aircraft of Aeroflot's International Directorate carried the title 'Official Olympic Carrier'. Back cover of Aeroflot's inflight magazine, No.1, 1980.

top right: Back cover of an Aeroflot promotional leaflet titled 'Welcome to the Caucasus', c.1979, showing the Olympic mascot Misha riding an Il-62.

bottom right: Double-folded greetings card, c.1980, with Olympic mascot Misha riding an Il-86.

above: Cigarette packet depicting an Ilyushin Il-18, 1960s.

right top: Presenting Aeroflot's 'one hundred different professions' in the national economy. Booklet published by Aviareklama, 1975.

right bottom: **Aeroflot – in the National Economy**. Booklet, c.1979.

The situation worsened on 1 September 1983, when a Soviet Air Force Sukhoi Su-15 shot down Korean Air Lines flight 007 travelling from New York to Seoul after the passenger jet mistakenly entered Soviet airspace. None of the 269 passengers survived. It was not until 29 April 1986 that flights between the USSR and the US were restored.

Despite these events, Aeroflot traffic via Shannon increased, with the airline channelling the entirety of its Central and South American operations through the airport. From 1983, Aeroflot was allowed to pay for all services at Shannon with fuel rather than money. The Soviets were delighted and duly increased fuel shipments from the Baltic port of Ventspils, allowing the Irish to sell Soviet fuel to other carriers.

Initially, Western airlines were suspicious of the quality of Soviet fuel: with its lower flash and freezing points (for cold climate use), its specifications did not correspond to the international standard. However, it was found to be just as safe as other fuel and any doubts were assuaged. Initially planning in 1980 to take 3 million gallons of

AEROFLOT
IN THE NATIONAL
ECONOMY

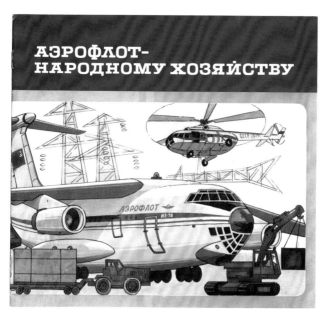

АЭРОФЛОТ-
НАРОДНОМУ ХОЗЯЙСТВУ

Северный Кавказ

АЭРОФЛОТ
Soviet airlines

above: **North Caucasus. Aeroflot**. Promotional booklet to entice both foreign and domestic tourists to the region, 1970s. The Hotel Tarelka at the Dombay ski resort was a Futuro house, designed in 1968 by Finnish architect Matti Suuronen. Fewer than 100 of these houses were constructed during the late 1960s and early 1970s. This particular Futuro still exists.

right: **Aeroflot**. Postcard, 1965.

Soviet fuel annually in exchange for services to Aeroflot at Shannon, this increased to almost 19 million gallons for 1,800 flights by 1989. From 1987, Aer Rianta made further deals with the USSR, including the painting and cabin refurbishment of Aeroflot's international directorate aircraft and the opening of the first duty-free shops at Moscow's Sheremetyevo airport.

By 1990, Aeroflot's network included 119 international destinations in more than 90 countries: 41 in Europe, 34 in Africa, 24 in Asia, eleven in the Middle East, six in South America and three in North America. Of those destinations, 114 were operated by the international directorate (Tsentral'noye Upravleniye Mezhdunarodnykh Vozdushnykh Soobshcheniy), working from Sheremetyevo in Moscow.

above: Bilingual Russian-English shopping bag (330 x 410 x 120 mm), 1970s.

top right: Model 58 shoulder bag (360 x 220 x 90 mm) decorated with a Tu-104. Made at Moscow leather factory No.3, 1965.

bottom right: Re-usable shopping bag (430 x 310 x 100 mm), 1980s.

Tu Aeroflot brochure cover with a Tupolev emblem and Tu-104 silhouette, 1961.

A flight attendant in front of a Tu-104 silhouette. East Siberian Directorate brochure, early 1960s.

9. CRASH LANDING

The break-up of the Soviet empire and its airline

While Aeroflot was able to fulfil its targets for the eleventh five-year plan (1981–85), Soviet economic stagnation had led to growing social unrest and attempts at political reform had failed to solve the problems. Relations with the US had deteriorated, leading to an increase in the military budget, with inevitable consequences for the civilian economy. The hopeless position of the Soviet Army in Afghanistan and the 1986 nuclear accident at Chernobyl further weakened the power of central government. As Soviet leader from 1985, Mikhail Gorbachev tried to speed up economic and social change with his *perestroika* (restructuring) and *glasnost* (openness) policies, including the radical Law on Co-operatives of May 1988, which permitted private ownership of businesses for the first time since the end of Lenin's New Economic Policy 60 years previously. Within months, the first new Soviet air carriers – independent of Aeroflot – began to appear.

The range of less profitable local flights dwindled to the point where routes were cancelled and small airfields closed. Dirt strips, once frequently used by Aeroflot planes, were now planted with crops, covered with apartment buildings or simply abandoned to nature. While passenger and freight figures kept rising, the tariffs for air services such as crop-spraying had doubled by 1987. This led to a significant cutback in contracts and a corresponding reduction in the amount of agricultural acreage treated, from 267 million acres in 1986 to 146 million in 1990.

Orders of new aircraft from Soviet manufacturers were delayed or, in some cases, not delivered at all and a lack of spare parts kept a significant proportion of the vast Aeroflot fleet on the ground. The airline also had to contend with fuel shortages and outdated technology and infrastructure, including overcrowded airports and deficiencies in air-traffic control. As operational standards deteriorated, flight safety was compromised.

On 24 August 1981, poor communication between military and civil air-traffic control caused a fatal accident for Aeroflot flight 811 (an Antonov An-24), en route from Komsomolsk-on-Amur to Blagoveshchensk in the Soviet far east. The plane, carrying 27 passengers and five crew members, was flying at 17,000 feet when it collided with an Air Force Tu-16 bomber carrying a crew of six. Both planes disintegrated, killing all but one of the passengers. Larisa

Добро пожаловать в Советский Союз!

Welcome to The Soviet Union! Kalinin Prospekt, Moscow. The famous Aeroflot Globe complete with Tu-144 (built in 1972) rotates above the Arbat Restaurant. *Aeroflot 82* magazine, 1982.

Savitskaya, a 21-year-old woman returning from her honeymoon, had been asleep in her seat at the back of the cabin when she was woken by the impact and a terrible burning sensation caused by the sudden drop in air pressure and temperature (from 25°C to minus 30°C). She became aware of a howling wind and the sound of screaming. The fuselage split open just in front of her and she was thrown into the aisle and against the tail bulkhead, which stunned her. Realising the plane had broken up and was falling, she struggled into a nearby window seat and braced herself. She recalled a flash of green before she hit the ground and lost consciousness – her impact had been softened by a small coppice of birch trees.

When she regained consciousness, she saw her dead husband opposite her, still in his seat. Despite suffering concussion, spinal injuries and multiple fractures, she was able to use the plane wreckage as a shelter, seat covers for warmth, a plastic bag for protection against mosquitoes and rainwater puddles to quench her thirst. She survived like this for three days before being found by the recovery team. It was later discovered that the 130 square foot piece of fuselage to which her seat was attached had buffeted down in a side-to-side motion (like the fall of a leaf) for eight minutes rather than gathering full and fatal momentum. She was paid compensation of 75 rubles (about £60 sterling), the standard award for non-permanently disabled survivors of such accidents.

On 20 October 1986, there was another shocking incident, this time involving Aeroflot flight 6502 Tu-134A (CCCP-65766) of the North-Caucasian Directorate, carrying 87 passengers and seven crew from Sverdlovsk (now Yekaterinburg) to Kuibyshev (now Samara). During the approach to Kuibyshev, the pilot in command bet his co-pilot that he could make an instrument-only 'blind' landing. In violation of all safety regulations, he had the cockpit curtains closed and ignored all instructions from the ground as well as the flight deck alarms. A moment before touchdown, he ordered the curtains to be opened, but it was too late and the Tupolev slammed on to the runway, destroying the left wing and causing the aircraft to roll over and burst into flames. Seventy people died including three flight attendants and the co-pilot, who collapsed from smoke inhalation while trying to rescue passengers. The pilot survived and was sentenced to a term in prison. Following this event, air crashes increasingly became the subject of public attention in the Soviet Union.

In addition to safety issues, inefficient airport security and a volatile political situation contributed to 33 hijackings in 1990 alone. As the political situation deteriorated, an increasing number of domestic flights were delayed for days or cancelled, while others were oversubscribed to the point where passengers were left without

Flight deck of a Tu-134, early 1970s.

seats. This led to a tragic incident on the morning of 1 August 1990, when Aeroflot flight E-35D – a Yak-40 (CCCP-87453) – took off from Yerevan (in the Armenian SSR) en route to Stepanakert (in the Azerbaijan SSR). On board were three crew members and 43 passengers, of whom only 30 were registered, with eleven having to stand in the aisle as the Yak-40 had seating for only 32 passengers.

Because of the overload, the pilot in command requested permission from air-traffic control to descend to a lower altitude and was allowed to fly at the minimum safe height of 14,750 feet. But navigational errors meant the crew lost sight of their position and gave the air-traffic controller at Stepanakert incorrect altitude information. Operating without radar, the controller permitted a further descent, and a minute later, at an altitude of 8,270 feet, the Yak-40 crashed into a cloud-covered mountain in the Karabakh range, some 14 miles west of their destination, killing all on board. This tragedy was followed by a similar one on 7 November 1991, when a Yak-40 (CCCP-87526) carrying four crew and 47 passengers – fifteen more than it was designed for – struck Kukurtbash mountain in poor visibility, killing everyone on board.

Aeroflot management tried to address the situation through a comprehensive internal reorganisation in which several directorates were transformed into independent airlines. With the Soviet civil aircraft industry unable to deliver new long-range aircraft, Aeroflot turned to the West, signing a contract with Airbus on 22 January 1990 for the lease of five A310-300s. By 1991, it was clear that the demands of an estimated 25 to 30 million Soviet air passengers could not be met by Aeroflot as a state-run entity and on 17 December, the USSR Ministry of Civil Aviation issued Order Number 287 'On the abolition of the USSR Ministry of Civil Aviation'.

A week later, on the morning of 25 December, Mikhail Gorbachev resigned as president of the USSR. He left the Kremlin that evening and the Soviet flag was lowered for the last time, marking the end of the Soviet Union. A few hours later, the Russian tricolour was raised, signalling the beginning of the Russian Federation. Each of the fifteen Soviet republics declared its independence and was recognised as a sovereign state; subsequently they all set up their own national airlines, with economic and legal autonomy from Aeroflot. Soviet Aeroflot's giant fleet of more than 11,000 aircraft, its airports, ground infrastructure and the personnel from the different directorates were divided between the republics and rebranded in the liveries of their new airlines.

The vast assets of an individual Soviet Republic's directorate would often be used to form a new 'national' airline, while other directorate fleets were shared between many entities, based on former divisions and subdivisions. This caused complications, particularly in the area of international flights. In the Soviet era, about 90 per cent of the country's international air traffic originated in Moscow, which meant most of the new airlines had no experience of regulations and commercial activity on international routes. Special agreements were made with the former International Directorate of Aeroflot – Soviet Airlines (Tsentral'noye Upravleniye Mezhdunarodnykh Vozdushnykh Soobshcheniy), with the result that the newly formed carriers continued for a transitional period to fly abroad under the Aeroflot flag, benefitting from Aeroflot's expertise and existing arrangements with other countries and airlines.

AEROFLOT'S PLANES

Promotional booklet, 1987. From front to back: Il-86, Il-62M, Tu-154B-2 and Tu-134A at Moscow Sheremetyevo airport.

The first Airbus A310-300 arrived at Moscow Sheremetyevo on 4 July 1992. This was the first Western airliner used by Aeroflot since the retirement of the Douglas C-47 from the fleet in the early 1950s. On 28 July, a new joint-stock company, named Aeroflot – Russian International Airlines (ARIA), was announced. It was the legal successor to Aeroflot – Soviet Airlines, inheriting the 103 airliners of the International Directorate (27 Il-62Ms, 19 Il-86s, 30 Tu-154s, 19 Il-76s, and eight Tu-134 A3s), along with its network of international air routes and its famous name and symbol.

A day later, Aeroflot's new Airbus A310 made its first commercial flight, drawing to a close the most remarkable era in civil aviation.

Embracing the Sky with Strong Arms.
Aeroflot connects more than 3,600 cities and settlements on the planet and carries more than 100 million passengers annually. Poster by A. Dobrov, 1983.

AFTERWORD

1992 to today

As the successor to Soviet Aeroflot's International Directorate, the new Aeroflot focused primarily on international flights from Moscow while the domestic market was dominated by so-called 'babyflots'. These were the many rapidly emerging airlines of the former Soviet Union, each attempting to organise its own operations. Since Aeroflot had been so vast and ubiquitous, this was not easy to accomplish. As Aeroflot's finance director Igor Desyatnichenko stated in late 1992: 'Consumers will buy a ticket that says Aeroflot on it and Aeroflot is written on the aircraft but the flight is operated by entities that are not connected with each other'. By the end of 1992, there were more than 60 airlines in the Russian Federation and 22 in the other former Soviet Republics.

This was a particularly chaotic period for Russian aviation. While the new airlines existed as separate companies on paper, their aircraft often still carried Aeroflot livery. Others bore hybrid colour schemes, and aircraft insignia could be painted in or out by hand overnight, as the need arose. Country designations on fuselages and under wings were treated in the same fashion, with CCCP covered by RA (for Russia) or UK (for Uzbekistan), and so on. New uniforms were slow to be issued and crew would arrive for work wearing old Aeroflot attire or their own clothing. Similarly, the old stock of Aeroflot tickets continued in service until new branded versions were printed. But this situation gradually changed as the new airlines' operations matured.

Economic instability, the continuous fall of the ruble and rising fuel prices affected every aspect of society and industry, including aviation. In 1994, air traffic in the former Soviet Union was 75 per cent lower than in 1990, despite the number of airlines growing to over 500 in the same period. More than 260 of these had been established from former branches of Aeroflot with another 120 growing from various sections of Soviet industry: large design bureaus, research bodies, ministries and industrial organisations that had been provided with their own aircraft to transport staff and materials. Another 50 or so were formed from military units while the remainder were genuinely new operations.

Once the economic situation had stabilised, Aeroflot was able gradually to expand its domestic network. In the year 2000, it carried a total of 5.1 million passengers, 1.4 million travelling on domestic routes (around 11 per cent of the domestic market). The company name was changed from Aeroflot – Russian International Airlines to Aeroflot – Russian Airlines to reflect the new emphasis. Economic growth boosted air traffic and on 14 April 2006, Aeroflot became the tenth member of the SkyTeam global airline alliance, enabling Aeroflot passengers to fly to any of the SkyTeam network's 728 destinations in 149 countries, to use SkyTeam airport lounges and to earn reward points within the bonus programmes of the alliance's other airlines.

As Aeroflot's fleet continued to expand and be renewed, Soviet aircraft were gradually phased out. On New Year's Eve 2009, the airline retired its last true Soviet-era airliner, a Tupolev 154M. The last Il-96 (developed in the Soviet Union but certified after its fall) was taken out of service on 30 March 2014.

As Russia's highest-ranking airline in terms of numbers of passengers, aircraft and routes, and because the Russian Federation owns a 51 per cent stake in it, Aeroflot – Russian Airlines is still considered to be the national air carrier. It forms the major part of the Aeroflot Group, Russia's largest airline holding company, alongside subsidiaries Rossiya and Aurora in the regional market and Pobeda in the low-cost carrier sector.

In 2019, the Aeroflot Group as a whole carried 60.7 million passengers on a young fleet of more than 350 modern aircraft, mainly of Boeing and Airbus manufacture, alongside the Russian-built Sukhoi Superjet 100. With further airliners under development and in production (such as the Irkut MS-21), the Russian civil aircraft industry is steadily regaining strength.

A century after the birth of Soviet civil aviation, Aeroflot – Russian Airlines carries on the legacy. Its crew uniforms and aircraft are still adorned with the winged hammer and sickle, proudly maintaining continuity with the great history of Soviet air travel.

overleaf: **For the Air Traveller. Aeroflot.** Leaflet, c.1960.

ВОЗДУШНОМУ

путешественнику

АЭРОФЛОТ

Bruno Vandermueren was born in 1977 and grew up in the vicinity of Brussels airport. From a young age he developed a keen interest in aviation and in 1998 he graduated with a degree in Aviation Technology from Ostend college. The airport of this Belgian coastal town was popular among aviation enthusiasts as in the 1990s it was a stopover for many of the newly formed Russian cargo airlines. It was here that the author photographed many of the former Aeroflot Ilyushin and Antonov planes. Since 1998, he has worked as an aircraft engineer and aircraft maintenance-operations coordinator for European Air Transport (DHL) and now TUI (Touristik Union International). Over the last 21 years, he has collected Soviet Aeroflot material, accumulating the largest collection in the world. He has flown on many Soviet aircraft and continues to travel to the former Soviet republics hunting for Aeroflot artefacts.

Published in 2021

FUEL Design & Publishing
33 Fournier Street
London E1 6QE

fuel-design.com

Design and edit by Murray & Sorrell FUEL
Copy edited by FUEL and Fergal Stapleton

Distribution by Thames & Hudson / D. A. P.
ISBN: 978-1-9162184-6-8
Printed in China